D0629468

# VISIT TO A SMALL PLANET

# Visit to a Small Planet

*by* GORE VIDAL

A COMEDY AKIN TO A VAUDEVILLE

Little, Brown and Company · BOSTON · TORONTO

Photographs by Courtesy of Fred Fehl



*Published simultaneously in Canada*
*by Little, Brown & Company (Canada) Limited*

PRINTED IN THE UNITED STATES OF AMERICA

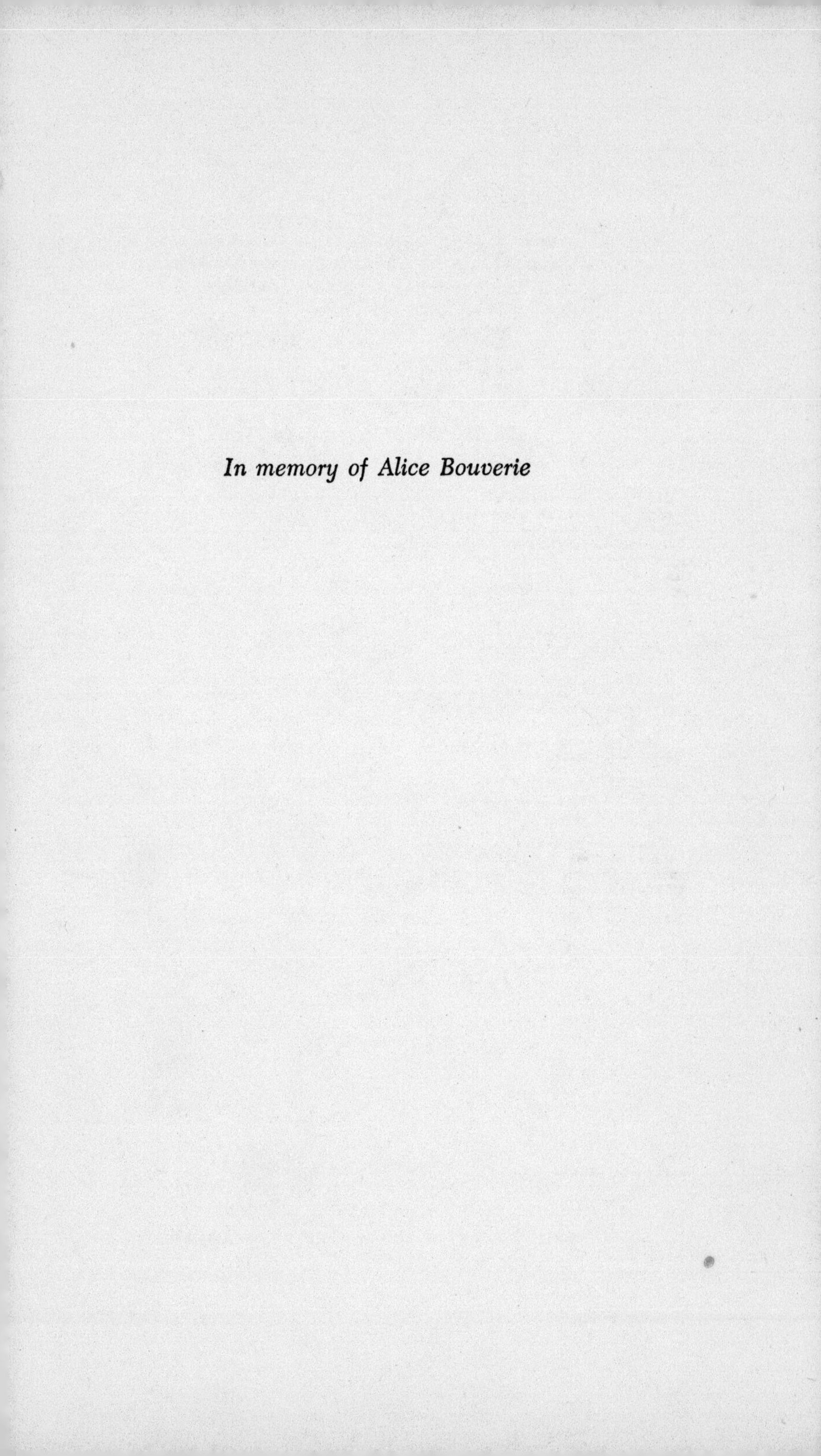

*In memory of Alice Bouverie*

# CONTENTS

The first performance of *Visit to a Small Planet* in New York City was given February 7, 1957 at the Booth Theatre. It was produced by George Axelrod and Clinton Wilder, and directed by Cyril Ritchard. Unusual sounds were created by Louis and Bebe Barron. The setting was by Oliver Smith, and the cast was as follows:

| | |
|---|---|
| KRETON | Cyril Ritchard |
| GENERAL TOM POWERS | Eddie Mayehoff |
| ROGER SPELDING | Philip Coolidge |
| ELLEN SPELDING | Sarah Marshall |
| CONRAD MAYBERRY | Conrad Janis |
| REBA SPELDING | Sibyl Bowan |
| AIDE | Robert Gothie |
| DELTON 4 | Francis Bethencourt |
| TWO TELEVISION TECHNICIANS | Earl Montgomery |
| | John Hallow |

The action of the play takes place in the house of Roger Spelding outside Manassas, Virginia. The time is next summer.

## ACT ONE

Early evening of a summer's day.

## ACT TWO

SCENE 1: The next morning.
SCENE 2: That evening.

## ACT THREE

An hour later.

# PREFACE

## PREFACE

### I

ONE SUNDAY, several theatrical seasons ago, I read with delight in the *New York Times* the furious demand of a not untalented playwright to be taken seriously. Outraged by the casual approbation of his judges, he declared that not only did he on occasion rise to lyricism but should anyone care to measure his first play against *Hamlet*, he would look no worse for the comparison. I found this vanity touching in its nakedness. The clown had cried out: "I am human! Love me!" But I also took malicious pleasure in a naïveté which reaffirmed my old conviction that writers in general . . . and minor playwrights in particular . . . are monsters of conceit, confident each of his own uniqueness, of the urgency of his vision.

As I put the paper down, I thought complacently of my good luck in having got so far beyond this prickly vanity. I had long ago decided that my occasional bad notices represented nothing more alarming than a temporary dereliction of taste on the part of overworked reviewers, while favorable comment was to be taken in stride as a heartening reminder that there was indeed an operative principle of justice in the world's affairs. I prided myself on a cool objectivity. Had I not survived more than a decade's exposure on the harsh steppes of the novel? There was nothing left to be said about my work. The best and the worst had already been recorded: no sudden savage thrust, no critical rudeness could penetrate a skin so cicatrized. But I was wrong (yes, I *am* approaching a point, but shyly): within days of my own theatrical debut, I found to my horror that I had fallen into the same terrible trap as the Sunday morning crybaby. I had been unmistakably impaled on the sharpened stake of vanity. Wreathed in critics' laurel—IT WAS NOT ENOUGH! I wanted to scream from the pit: *You must take me seriously!* Maddened as I am. I cannot make my colleague's other complaints: though oppressed and tiny, the voice of sanity does assure me that I have not endangered *Hamlet's* place in the canon of the drama nor do I . . . and it must be faced squarely . . . rise to lyricism. Yet I am *not* content to be regarded as one of the many who trot so merrily through the market place, wearing bright motley, diffident bells tinkling. Rather, I see myself as Tamburlaine approaching Persepolis, and I have experienced a flesh-bursting urge to establish my own primacy (and why else is this sort of preface ever written?) in the inconsequential shadow world of the theatre.

But before I rearrange the hierarchy of comedy to afford myself a central place, I must confess right off that I am not at heart a playwright. I am a novelist turned temporary adventurer; and I chose to write television, movies, plays for much the same reason that Captain Morgan selected the Spanish Main for his peculiar . . . and not dissimilar . . . sphere of operations. The reasons for my conversion to piracy are to me poignant, and to students of our society perhaps significant. If I may recall in nostalgic terms the near past, I did, as a novelist, enjoy a bright notoriety after the Second World War. Those were the happy years when a new era in our letters was everywhere proclaimed; we would have, it was thought, a literature to celebrate the new American empire; our writers would reflect our glory and complement the beautiful hardness of our currency. But something went wrong. The new era did not materialize and the work of my generation was finally dismissed . . . for now at least . . . as a false dawn.

And it *is* a fact that the novel as a popular art form retrogressed gravely in our reign. Not clever enough to interest the better critics, nor simple enough to divert the public, we lost the critics to pure criticism and the public to impure television. By the 1950's I and my once golden peers were plunged into that dim cellar of literature characterized as "serious" where, like the priests of a shattered establishment, we were left to tend our prose privately . . . so many exiles, growing mushrooms in the dark.

The passage of time has only confirmed the new order. Less and less often is that widening division between the commercially viable and the seriously meaningful bridged by the rare creator who is both. Most of the publishing events of recent years have been the crudely recollected experiences of nonwriters. Apparently obliterated is the antique conception of the man of letters creating a life's work to be enjoyed by the common reader in continuity. True, that nineteenth-century phenomenon never quite took root in this country, and lovely though New England's Indian summer was, winter, when it came, was killing; nowadays our better literary men seek refuge in the universities, leaving what is left of the public novel to transient primitives and to sturdy hacks. Nor, let me say, are the serious writers themselves responsible for their unpopularity as our more chauvinistic editorial writers would have it. The good work of the age is being done, as always. Rather, it is the public which has changed. Television, movies, the ease of travel, so many diversions have claimed the attention of the old reading public and it is doubtful if ever again the novel will have the enormous prestige, the universal audience it had at that golden moment when an idler on a Mississippi wharf shouted to the pilot of a passing steamer: "Is Little Nell dead?" And, alas, Mistah Kurtz, he dead, too . . . solemnly embalmed by the Academy.

Today, the large audience holds communion in a new, more compelling establishment. I doubt if many Americans could identify a single character in a work of modern fiction, but there are few who could not describe in exact detail the night on television when Charles Van Doren failed to identify the King of the Belgians. And it is vain to deplore a cultural change. After two pre-eminent centuries, the novel no longer is useful to the public . . . yet only novelists need mourn, for it is a fact of civilization that each society creates the games it wants to play. And though the main audience has turned back to the play (in all its various forms, both "live" and filmed) it is, nevertheless, a stoic consolation for those of us whose first allegiance is the novel to know that there will always be some serious interest in one's work, that the keys to the kingdom of prose will continue to be passed on from hand to hand. And though I rather suspect that in a century's time the novel will be as rare and private an art form as poetry today or that delicate and laborious process by which dedicated men fire glass with color, it will always be worth the doing.

II

There are of course compensations in any defeat. There is the sense of a hard duty done, and in the case of the artist who has become unfashionable or . . . worse still . . . whose art form has collapsed beneath him, there is an obvious grandeur in holding fast to the high altar as ominous fissures in the earth open and the columns fall. In one sense, I await oblivion with a martyr's complacency; it pleases me to write novels and I shall continue to the end, with or without readers. But making enough money to live presents a problem, and since I am not clever enough to go into business (much the wisest course for anyone who wants to be a serious writer . . . if only because one's literary faculties are not exploited by the day's work) I was forced to learn a trade. I chose play-writing. It did not tap the same sources of energy as novel-writing. It was highly remunerative and if one bothered to take it seriously, it could provide a marvelous megaphone through which to trumpet those fancies and irritable crotchets one would like the many to heed.

Over the years, I attempted three stage plays. When I was nineteen, I wrote a quasi-poetic work about, Heaven alone knows why, a man who became a werewolf, in Manhattan. I destroyed all copies of this early effort only to learn recently that a collector had somehow got hold of a copy, a ghastly prospect for some as yet unborn English major. The next play was on an equally obscure subject, written in a Pindaric frenzy in the spring of 1948 at Shepheard's Hotel in Cairo. Later that summer, I gave it to Tennessee Williams to read. He pronounced it the worst play he'd read in some time, and I abandoned play-writing for good . . . I thought . . . after first pointing out to him that a literary form which depended on the combined excellence of others for its execution could hardly be worth the attention of a serious writer, adding with deliberate cruelty that I did not envy him being stage-struck, his life taken up with such ridiculous people as actors and directors. He agreed that I should not expose myself just yet to this sort of tedium.

Six years later, driven by necessity, I took the plunge into television, the very heart of darkness, and to my surprise found that I liked it, that it could be taken seriously, and that in spite of the many idiot restrictions imposed by those nervous sponsors who pay for plays, it was possible to do a certain amount of satisfactory work. The thought, too, of a mass audience was awesome. New novels are not wanted. They are written because one wants to write them and that is that. But television needed plays by the hundreds. I don't think there has been anything comparable since the Elizabethan theatre, when new plays were turned out with rich abandon to keep resident companies busy (no further comparison, of course, is possible!).

Yet despite its raw youth there is a tradition already firmly established in television that comedies seldom work and that satire *never* does. Like most traditions this one is founded on a small truth. For one thing, the comedy timing of stage-trained actors is inevitably affected by the absence of human response during a performance, and for another, several people sitting at home glumly staring at a television set are not apt to find anything very amusing unless it is heavily underscored by laughter from a studio audience. And plays on television are performed without audiences. Satire presents a further difficulty for the mass audience. If satire is to be effective, the audience must be aware of the thing satirized; if they are not, the joke falls flat. Unfortunately for our native satirists, the American mass audience possess very little general information on any subject. Each individual knows his own immediate world, but as various research polls continually inform us, he holds little knowledge in common with others. Even political jokes, were they allowed on television, would not have much relevance. Recently one national poll discovered that almost half of those queried could not identify the Secretary of State. The size of the population of course has much to do with this collective ignorance. When Aristophanes made a satiric point, he could be confident that his audience would appreciate his slyest nuance because in a small community each citizen was bound to share with his fellows a certain amount of general information, literary, religious, and political. National units today are too large and, in America at least, education is too bland to hope for much change. As a result, satire, unless done very broadly, like that of Mr. Al Capp, our national Hogarth (or the playing version of *Visit to a Small Planet*), puzzles and irritates rather than amuses.

I have often thought that the domination of naturalism in our letters is directly attributable to the breakdown of the old homogeneous American society of the nineteenth century by, variously, the influx of immigration, the discovery of exciting new machinery, the ease of travel. . . . Yet before this burst of population and invention, an educated man, writing allusively, could assume that his readers would respond knowledgeably to a fairly large number of references both literary and social. Since 1900 this has been less and less possible, and it is no coincidence that naturalism should be to this day the preferred manner in the novel if only because the naturalistic writer, by definition, takes nothing for granted. He assumes the reader knows no more than he chooses to tell. He constructs a literal world of concrete detail. His narrative is easily followed. He records the surface of life with a photographer's care, leaving the interpretation, the truth of his record to the reader's imagination: the result is that our time's most successful *popular* writing, aesthetically, is journalism . . . another dagger at the novel's heart.

## III

The idea for *Visit to a Small Planet* was rejected by three television sponsors before the Philco-Goodyear Playhouse bought it. I was told that the advertisers found the premise alarming, which was certainly disingenuous of them. Had I not spun my fragile satire about the one glittering constant in human affairs, the single pastime which never palls: war? In fact, one might say that *Visit* is the happiest of pro-war plays. But only Philco saw the austere beauty of my conceit, and on the night of May 8, 1955 it was telecast. With some anxiety, we waited for the roof to fall in; to our very real surprise it did not, and most people were pleased with my gentle heresy. I suspect it was Cyril Ritchard's fine performance which did most of the pleasing, but that was to be expected.

I was then informed that George Axelrod would like me to do a stage version which he himself would produce. And so it came to pass. Expansion was not difficult. As a novelist, I am accustomed to using a hundred thousand words to net my meaning. My problem theatrically has always been one of compression; left to myself, I go on and on. After the script was ready there were the usual trials, delays, problems of temperament: each participant confident the others had gone into secret league to contrive his professional ruin (and on occasion cabals did flourish . . . the theatre is a child's world).

On January 16, 1956 the play opened in New Haven. From that moment until the New York opening on February 7 I was more dentist than writer, extracting the sharper (but not always carious) teeth. The heart of the play's argument was a scene in the second act between Kreton and the Secretary-General of the United Nations. At each performance the audience, which had been charmed by the precedent fooling, grew deathly cold as the debate began: this was not what they had anticipated (a fault, I own, of the dramaturgy . . . were I a better playwright the scene would have developed inevitably) and their confidence in the play was never entirely regained. A few days before we left Boston, I replaced the scene with a lighter one, involving the principals and giving the curtain to our subtlest player, the cat. The substitute was engaging; the play moved amiably; no one was shocked (some observers in New Haven had declared the entire conception unwholesomely menacing). And so by deliberately dulling the edge of the satire, the farce flourished, giving rise to the misapprehension that the evening was delightful largely because of the comedic improvisations of two gifted *farceurs*. Our clowns were certainly gifted, but if I may be predictable and come to the defense of my squat but healthy child, they did *not* create, they played. The comedic invention was mine.

A number of reviewers described the play as a vaudeville, a very apt description, and one in which I concur, recalling a letter from Bernard Shaw to Granville Barker: "I have given you a series of first-rate music hall entertainments thinly disguised as plays, but really offering the public a unique string of turns by comics and serio-comics of every popular type." That of course is only half the truth, but it is the charming half. In the case of *Visit* the comedic approach to the theme tended to dictate the form. Having no real commitment to the theatre, no profound convictions about the well-made or the ill-made play, I tend to write as an audience, an easily bored audience. I wrote the sort of piece I should like to go to a theatre to see; one in which people say and do things that make me laugh. And though vague monsters lurk beneath the surface, their presence is sensed rather than dramatically revealed. My view of reality is not sanguine and the play for all its blitheness turns resolutely toward a cold night. But happily for the play's success, the incisors were extracted out of town and the venture was a hit. But there in that word "hit" lies the problem.

I was obliged to protect an eighty-thousand-dollar investment and I confess freely that I obscured meanings, softened blows, humbly turned wrath aside, emerging, as we all wanted, with a successful play which represents me very little . . . perhaps a good thing. It is not that what was fashioned is bad or corrupt. I rather fancy the farce we ended up with, and I think it has a good deal of wear in it. But the play that might have been, though hardly earth-shaking, was far more interesting and true.

But although like my poor stung colleague who wanted to be taken seriously, I too feel hurt at the sort of reputation which hovers about my part of this venture, I cannot honestly make much of a case for myself. I played the game stolidly according to rules I abhor. But in extenuation I should like to say what many others have said before me: the theatre and its writers are seriously, perhaps fatally, hampered by economic pressure. Because it costs too much to put on a play, one works in a state of hysteria. Everything is geared to success. Yet art is mostly failure. And it is only from a succession of daring, flawed works that the occasional masterwork comes. But in our theatre to fail is death and the author of a play which fails is regarded with much the same sympathy as the murderer of a child. In an atmosphere so feverish it is difficult to work with objectivity. Only the honest hacks have a good time of it. Cannily, they run up a banner: It's just us again, kids, trying to make a buck. And they are let off with genial contempt. It is the crankier, more difficult writers who must work at a disadvantage, and efforts to divert them into familiar safe channels are usually disastrous.

But things are as they are. No time has been easy for any of the arts. And, to take the longest view, one must recall that society does not exist for the express purpose of creating literature . . . a hard fact for many of us to realize. When certain forms lose their usefulness, they are discarded. It may be that the novel was a temporary diversion . . . less than three centuries old in English . . . and that the play, thanks to social changes and new machinery, has regained its ancient ascendancy. As for myself, I am divided at heart. I should never have been drawn to playwriting had it been possible to live by prose. Yet what I began in a fit of opportunism, I have persisted in with some pleasure, at least in the actual work. Nor am I displeased with this unexpected change in course, for have I not, like one of those civilizations Professor Toynbee so enjoys inventing, risen to a desperate challenge and survived? — at least for now. But the main thing, finally, is not the means by which work is accomplished, prose or dramaturgy, but the sense of life imparted. To one's own view is the commitment, not to the form which contains it. In this particular work, I turned to comedy for the stage because it seemed to me the best means I had at hand to pursue the elusive whole. What is to follow? I don't dare guess, but perhaps (oh, impossible challenge!) I shall one day . . . in the phrase of my fellow clown . . . rise to lyricism.

# VISIT TO A SMALL PLANET

# ACT ONE

## ACT ONE

*The curtain rises on the colonial porch, living room and study (from stage right to left) of Roger Spelding's house near Manassas, Virginia.*

*It is a sultry summer evening, not yet dark. On the porch are wrought-iron chairs and a swing. Trees, full-foliaged, stop the view.*

*The living room is comfortable, expensive. In one corner (downstage right) of the living room is a television set, arranged so that the audience cannot make out the picture.*

*The study is businesslike with a table desk — Second Empire. Nearby, there is a large globe on a stand.*

*In the living room are Roger Spelding and Major General Tom Powers. Roger Spelding is a confident middle-aged man with a receding hairline and an odd double manner: when he is being a television commentator, he is warm, folksy, his accent faintly Southern; when he is himself, the accent is more national, the tone more acerb and sophisticated.* A faux bonhomme.

*General Powers is the same age, an adept politician of the services, devoted to his own advancement, which has not been as rapid as he'd anticipated. He ascribes all setbacks to treachery in high places.*

*Powers is at the moment distraught.*

POWERS

. . . and I'm in charge. It's all mine. All of it. The whole insane mess. Of course, when it first broke, it was strictly Strat. Air's baby. Nobody could get near it. Cover them with glory, they thought. Ha! But yesterday Lieutenant General Claypoole decided it was too hot for him to handle, so while my back was turned with the new Laundry Project — something really exciting, by the way (ROGER *offers* POWERS *a cigar*) — thank you, Rog — Strat. Air tosses it to Major General Spotty McClelland — he's Com. Air Int. now — who lobs it straight at me; so by the time I get back from luncheon, I find I've been TD'd C.O.S. Priority-1A the hell and gone out of Interserv. Strat. Tac. into Kangaroo Red with the whole bloody UFO deal dumped right in my lap. (ROGER *lights* POWERS' *cigar, then* ROGER *crosses upstage to a console on which is placed a portable bar.* POWERS *distractedly follows him* ) Thank you, Rog. *While* Lieutenant General Claypoole *and* my good friend Major General Spotty McClelland are sitting there in the Chief of Staff's air-conditioned office sucking up to those damned civilians: "Yes, Mr. Secretary. No, Mr. Secretary. It's only an invasion from Mars or something, Mr. Secretary." So why not let good old Tom Powers handle it? Of course, if he goofs, he can always go back to Panama! (*He pulls himself together with an effort* ) Sorry, Roger. I shouldn't be talking like this. But they mean to destroy me.

(ROGER *pours* POWERS *a stiff drink* )

ROGER

It's okay, Tom boy. I didn't understand a word you said. *What* has been dumped in your lap?

POWERS

UFO. You know, U.F.O. — Unidentified Flying Objects. Flying saucers. (*Indicates the bottle of soda in* ROGER's *hands* ) Right to the top, Rog. Claypoole knows damn well I come up for promotion to permanent B.G. in January and . . .

ROGER

*(Contemptuously)*

*A flying saucer?* Oh, come off it, Tom boy. As I prove to my television audience tonight, there "jest" ain't no "sech" animal. No, sir. No "sech" animal.

(ROGER *crosses to the sofa and sits down.* POWERS *joins him*)

POWERS

*(Officially)*

Two days ago an unidentified object appeared in the earth's atmosphere. For the last twelve hours it has been observed over Washington and this part of Virginia.

ROGER

*(Hard-hitting, shrewd)*

Are you sure this isn't an Air Force stunt? You know, get a bigger appropriation out of Congress . . .

POWERS

*(Patiently)*

Roger, I've seen the thing myself.

ROGER

*(Promptly)*

Optical illusion . . . mass hysteria . . .

POWERS

Now, Roger, this is strictly confidential. I'm telling you this as an old and trusted friend, not as (*A nervous look to left and right*) a television commentator: Whatever it is it's real—*registers on your radar.*

ROGER

But if it's real, I . . . (*Sudden horror*) Tom! My telecast . . . it's on film! In just fifteen minutes I'll be telling Mother and Father America that there "jest" ain't no "sech" . . . Oh, my God. I'll call the studio. I'll make an announcement . . .

POWERS

(*Shakes his head, rising*)

Sorry, Roger. This is classified, pending final clearance as top secret.

ROGER

(*Losing temper*)

Suppose I break the story anyway? It's a free country . . .

POWERS

(*Coolly*)

You'd be indicted under the Revised Espionage Act. I'm sorry, Roger.

ROGER

(*Into phone*)

Get me New York . . .

(REBA SPELDING, *a vague, gray woman, beneath whose gentleness glints the iron will of the faddist, enters from the hall*)

REBA

Tom Powers from the Harvard Business School! Look at you! All filled out and everything . . . and an admiral, too! (*To* ROGER) I wouldn't have recognized him!

ROGER

He's a general. He's in the Army.

(*Gives up on the telephone*)

POWERS

Gosh, it's grand to see you, Reba, really grand. Why, Roger, this little lady hasn't changed one iota in twenty years.

REBA

Oh, Tom, that isn't true! Remember my hair? (*She spins gaily around* ) Well, *look!* It's so much longer now. See? Anyway, you come on upstairs and I'll show you your room and . . .

POWERS

I'm sorry, Reba. Can't stay. Just passing through. (*Examines watch*) They expect me in Manassas at nineteen hundred.

ROGER

He's on a mission.

REBA

(*Disappointed*)

A mission? In Virginia? And I thought you were here to see us. Roger, where's Ellen? I want Tom to meet her.

ROGER

(*With distaste*)

Off somewhere with Conrad, the boy farmer.

REBA

(*To* POWERS)

Well, you come to dinner tonight, and we'll have a real reunion.

POWERS

Tell you what I'll do, Reba (*Thoughtful pause*), I'll do my best. (*Crosses to* ROGER) Roger, it's grand seeing you, but remember (*Lowers his voice*), this flying saucer business is *top secret.*

REBA

(*Overhearing*)

Flying saucer? Oh, but there aren't any flying saucers; Roger says there aren't. In fact, tonight he's going to prove it's all in the mind . . .

POWERS

Will you just come out here, folks? (*Leads them onto the porch and downstage. He points straight up* ) You see? Way up there? To the left of that tree? Not to the right . . . the *left* of that tree. Well, that's it.

REBA

(*With wonder*)

Why, there *is* something way up there. Tom's perfectly right.

ROGER

*(Putting on glasses)*

*I* can't see a thing.

REBA

Those are your *reading* glasses. What did you say it was, Tom?

POWERS

An unidentified flying object.

REBA

*(Pleased)*

Oh, yes. *Yes*. Of course. That's exactly what it looks like.

POWERS

*(Napoleon leaving Russia)*

And it's mine . . . all mine. And I was so happy in the Laundry Corps at Interserv. Strat. Tac. Well, that's the way the ball bounces.

*(Walks off muttering)*

REBA

*(Calling brightly after him)*

Dinner at eight.

*(*ROGER *gazes blankly at sky. Then he turns disgustedly and goes back into the living room)*

ROGER

Mass hysteria. A simple case of mass hysteria.

*(*REBA *follows him)*

REBA

It's really rather pretty, whatever it is. (*Her thought changes abruptly, as it is wont to do* ) Roger, do you think Ellen's sleeping with Conrad?

(ROGER *stares at her; disaster looms before his eyes*)

ROGER

There must be some way of killing that broadcast.

(REBA *settles down on the sofa for a comfortable monologue. She takes out her knitting*)

REBA

If she is, I just hope they don't do anything silly . . . you know, like getting married.

ROGER

Maybe I could get them to run an old film. One of my "Open Letters to the American Mom" . . . or one of those damned "Tolerance" things.

REBA

It's not that I don't like Conrad. I do. But Ellen must finish college.

ROGER

(*Glumly*)

No. Too late to get union clearance . . .

REBA

Roger, I wish you'd take more interest in your daughter. You never talk to her.

ROGER

*(Checking in)*

She could hear me on television three nights a week, if she'd take the trouble. . . . It can't be a flying saucer. It just can't.

REBA

*My* father always talked to me. He used to read aloud, too. You *never* read aloud.

ROGER

*(Flames approach the stake)*

This is going to be another Thomas E. Dewey. I can feel it coming. Oh, when you've got a Trendex like mine, you've got enemies, waiting for you to fall on your face; nine years and they still haven't forgotten. (*Shudders at the memory*) Millions of people heard that broadcast: "Congratulations," I said, "congratulations, President Dewey!"

*(A bitter, mocking laugh)*

REBA

My father met Dewey once. It was right after he came back from Manila.

ROGER

And tonight, "Mother and Father America — Take it from yours truly, Roger Spelding: there jest ain't no sech animal. . . ."

*(With a cry of self-loathing, goes off up the stairs, muttering)*

(REBA *continues placidly with her knitting.* ELLEN *and* CONRAD *run onto the porch.* CONRAD *embraces her apishly; they settle on the swing downstage and engage in desultory love-making.* CONRAD *is an ordinary-looking youth, more earnest than serious.* ELLEN *is a splendid girl of nineteen, iron-willed but appealing* )

ELLEN

( *Mildly reluctant* )

No . . . no, that's enough, Conrad, stop . . . please.

CONRAD

I can't. ( *He takes her in his arms again* ) There's some terrible force driving me on and on and on . . .

ELLEN

( *Pushes him away* )

Well, you just restrain that terrible force, because I'm getting prickly heat again. ( *She reveals the nape of her neck* ) See? Here.

CONRAD

Where?

ELLEN

All up and down.

CONRAD

Oh, no. That's not prickly heat. That's me. I didn't shave.

( *He demonstrates by rubbing his face against her neck: a wily, manly ruse* )

ELLEN

( *Sighing* )

Conrad, don't! You're disfiguring me. . . . I wonder who that was with Daddy just now. I thought I heard him say . . .

CONRAD

I don't see how anybody can make love and eavesdrop at the same time. Do one or the other, but don't . . .

ELLEN

(*Contrite*)

It's awful—the way I'm always doing two things at once. Sometimes three. I lack depth. I know it. They think I'm shallow at Bryn Mawr.

CONRAD

Well, I find you charming, in your shallow way.

ELLEN

You're sweet.

(*He looks long and tenderly into her face*)

CONRAD

(*Softly*)

Oh, hell, the goat. (*Glances at watch*) I got to go home. Time for her medicine.

ELLEN

I'm beginning to resent that goat.

CONRAD

It's not her fault she's sick.

ELLEN

And she resents me. No, really. I think it's a very peculiar coincidence that when I got back from school, inflamed by your passionate postcards, that goat went into a physical decline and had to be moved into your house, into your *one-room* house, making it impossible for me to set foot in there, much less . . . pay a real call. She's faking, I tell you. She's expressing her hostility toward me.

CONRAD

Honey, it's only temporary.

ELLEN

No, it all seems to be part of some diabolic plan to keep us apart. First, the goat moved into your house. Then, last night . . .

(*She pauses, recollected horror on her face*)

CONRAD

You still upset about us getting thrown out of that motel?

ELLEN

It was awful.

CONRAD

(*A surge of guilt*)

I'm sorry. I lost my head.

ELLEN

(*Ruthlessly*)

You became panicky. No luggage . . .

CONRAD

I could've sworn I had a suitcase in the back of the car.

ELLEN

And no reservation. The way that man looked at us, I felt . . . sordid. And that name you signed . . .

CONRAD

I blacked out.

ELLEN

That was no excuse for writing "Mr. and Mrs. Ulysses Simpson Grant *and wife.*" (*He cringes. She sighs, then she rises and stretches like a cat* ) Oh, I wish something would happen! Something different. I feel I'm just drifting.

CONRAD

Well, what do you *want* to do?

ELLEN

If I knew, I wouldn't be drifting. But something important. Like saving the world . . . or helping out in a flood.

CONRAD

You'll have plenty to do on the farm. (*He stretches out on the swing* ) The natural life. No foreign entanglements.

ELLEN

But suppose there's another war? Daddy keeps saying there's going to be one. Practically any minute.

CONRAD

Not for us, there won't.

ELLEN

But you'd have to go.

CONRAD

I'd go to jail first.

(*He pulls her toward him*)

ELLEN

Didn't you like the last war?

CONRAD

No. That's why I'm a farmer and a pacifist and . . . Oh, honey, I'm in love with you. (*Kisses her*) Marry me. Right now.

(*She pulls away*)

ELLEN

As you may have suspected, Conrad, I find you "sexually attractive," but . . . well, you don't have any . . . money.

CONRAD

I don't happen to believe in money.

ELLEN

I don't think that helps. Anyway, I'm still too immature to know my own mind. You see, I want you and money and connubial bliss and a college degree and a little diamond tiara — you know, like they wear in the ballet —

CONRAD

Honey, be simple.

(*He kisses her and she responds warmly*)

ELLEN

(*Completing her thought*)

And I want to be simple, too. I suppose that's the one thing I really am and don't know it.

(REBA, *in the living room, puts down her knitting and goes out onto portico. Unaware of the lovers, she studies the sky*)

CONRAD

We could have such a wonderful life over there on the farm, and you'd be right next door to your father, who hates me.

ELLEN

You're hypersensitive.

CONRAD

He hates me.

ELLEN

No, darling, he *dislikes* you. But he doesn't like anybody very much; that's why he's such a wonderful news analyst.

(*They are now happily intertwined on the swing as* REBA *discovers them*)

REBA

There you are, Ellen. (CONRAD *jumps to his feet* ) Hello, Conrad. (*To* ELLEN) I wondered where you were. Well, you'll never guess who was here! Tom Powers.

ELLEN

Who?

REBA

Admiral Powers. He was with your father at the Harvard Business School and now he's over in Manassas with the Army doing something about that flying saucer.

ELLEN

(*Bemused*)

An admiral in the Army?

REBA

Exactly what I said, but your father explained it.

CONRAD

What's that about a flying saucer?

REBA

It seems there is one, after all. It's way up there.

(*Points*)

See, right above that tulip tree, the one the woodpeckers killed. Pretty, isn't it?

CONRAD

(*Alarmed*)

My God, look at that thing!

ELLEN

How bright it is!

CONRAD

(*To* REBA)

What did the admiral say it was?

REBA

I told you — an unidentified flying object. (*Starts to straighten* ELLEN's *skirt: sudden suspicion*) What have you two been up to all afternoon?

ELLEN

Conrad asked me to marry him again.

REBA

(*Firmly*)

No.

CONRAD

Hey, look, there it goes. . . . Now it's gone.

REBA

Oh, good. Daddy was right, after all. We're suffering from mass hysteria, just like he said.

(REBA *sits on the bench*)

CONRAD

(*Turning away*)

It's probably one of those weather balloons.

REBA

(*To* ELLEN)

Ellen, no marriage till we finish college and get our degree. (*To* CONRAD) Conrad, nowadays a girl needs more than one string on her bow. Marriage isn't enough. *I* know . . . how well I know! I wanted to be a dietitian when I was a girl—now don't laugh, I'm quite serious. Oh, I realize it sounds ambitious, but I was that sort of girl: I wanted to be something useful. But then I married Mr. Spelding and of course . . .

ELLEN

Mother, I'm majoring in art appreciation. That's not very useful.

REBA

How do you know? Suppose there was a depression?

ELLEN

And I want to have lots of children. I appreciate children a lot more than art.

REBA

You mustn't talk like this in front of Conrad.

ELLEN

But it's true. Anyway, it's all I'm fit for. (*Gloomily*) Breeding. A broad pelvis. Out in the fields. Then, an hour later, back to the plow, carrying my newborn child on my back . . . or do they just leave it in the fields?

REBA

(*Shocked*)

Ellen! If you're going to talk like that, go some place where smart talk's appreciated. Go to a bar or . . . or to a bus station. And when I think of all the work I did with poor Margaret Sanger! The lectures we gave! The leaflets we distributed. (*She rises and crosses to* CONRAD.) Conrad, I appeal to you! The world can't feed the people in it already, much less these new ones coming along every minute.

CONRAD

Well, I have my farm.

REBA

I'll see if I can find some of Margaret's pamphlets. She'll frighten you to death, all those statistics . . . (*She starts to go, then pauses*) You two aren't going to do anything silly, are you?

ELLEN

(*Sighs*)

No, Mother.

REBA

Good. Dinner's at eight. We're expecting you, Conrad. (*She goes into living room* ) I sometimes wonder if all that cod liver oil wasn't a mistake. (*Sadly, she goes out through the hall, talking* ) Cod liver oil for this, cod liver oil for that: children were stuffed with it and now look at them!

(ELLEN *and* CONRAD *look at one another thoughtfully* )

CONRAD

I'd like a big family.

ELLEN

So would I.

CONRAD

Let's start . . . right now. (*He takes her, but she pulls away*) What're you thinking about?

ELLEN

A little diamond tiara . . .

CONRAD

Not on my farm.

(*He embraces her fiercely, throwing her off balance. They fall onto the swing, where they remain, torn between laughter and lust.* ROGER SPELDING *appears from upstairs, carrying binoculars. He stops when he sees them. He peers nearsightedly at* ELLEN, *who is unaware of him*)

ELLEN

(*Giggling*)

Oh, Conrad! Conrad, stop! Conrad!

ROGER

(*Curiously*)

Ellen? That *is* you, isn't it?

(CONRAD *springs to his feet, an ingenuous boyish smile on his young satyr lips*)

ELLEN

(*Embarrassed*)

Yes, Daddy.

CONRAD

Hi, Mr. Spelding.

ROGER

(*Hate*)

Conrad.

CONRAD

Mr. Spelding, we were just . . .

ROGER

I understand — perfectly.

(*He starts back into the house. At the door he stops and glances back over his shoulder at* CONRAD. *With a small grimace of distaste, he goes back into the house, into the study, where he takes down a book, sits at his desk and ponders*)

CONRAD

He hates me. . . . Now, honey, you know that new motel on Route 9? The Jefferson Davis? Well, at this very moment they are holding Cottage D for a Mr. and Mrs. — and get this for a name — Claude Ollinger of Bethesda, Maryland.

ELLEN

What a dreary name!

CONRAD

Sure, it's dreary; that's the whole point. It has the dreary ring of truth. I also plan to carry a duffel bag, and if you really want to go wild, I'll bring my foot locker, too. Why not? Spend the whole week end.

(ELLEN *makes her decision*)

ELLEN

Are you sure you won't go to pieces when the man asks you to sign that funny name?

CONRAD

I swear. Baptism of fire.

ELLEN

Are you absolutely sure you can spell "Ollinger?" (CONRAD *nods*) And you'll bring a respectable-looking suitcase, a small one?

(*Tension gathers. The future is evident*)

CONRAD

I will. I see the Ollingers as owners of a small, kind of green-looking bag, with a zipper. It won't be empty, either. I'll weigh it down with telephone books.

ELLEN

(*Taking the plunge*)

All right, darling. Tonight. After dinner. We'll say we're going to . . . the movies. I don't know why I suddenly feel so nervous.

CONRAD

Neither do I. After all, we're getting married soon.

ELLEN

I'm not so sure about that. Well, anyway. (*Briskly*) Go home. Change. Mother the goat.

CONRAD

See you, honey.

(*He kisses her briefly and starts to go. She calls after him: a second thought*)

ELLEN

(*The organizational mind*)

And when you come back, leave the bag *in* the car! (*She looks at the house nervously; she lowers her voice* ) I mean, don't bring it in to dinner, or anything.

(CONRAD *laughs and goes*)

ELLEN

(*To herself*)

Mr. and Mrs. Claude Ollinger, of Bethesda, Maryland.

(*She sighs, half pleased, half anxious*)

ROGER

(*Shutting book*)

The planet Venus is covered with ammonia. And there's nothing but fungus on Mars. The Air Force is behind this. I knew it. I just knew it.

(*The clock chimes seven o'clock.* ROGER *rises and enters the living room, turning on lights: it is now evening*)

ROGER

(*Calls upstairs*)

Reba! Seven o'clock. Time to listen to me.

(*He crosses to the television set as* ELLEN, *bemused, enters*)

ELLEN

Daddy, should I marry for love or money?

ROGER

(*He adjusts dials*)

Money.

(REBA *enters from the hall*)

REBA

Ellen, I found one of Margaret's pamphlets. And it's a *shocker.*

ROGER

Now the damn sound won't work.

(REBA *settles down comfortably to watch*)

REBA

Oh, now, Roger. Anyway, we can *see* you. Then you can tell us what you said when it's over.

(ROGER *groans but he sits down beside* REBA. *He studies his performance critically.* ELLEN *daydreams on the sofa. A long moment*)

REBA

(*Thoughtfully*)

You look tired.

ROGER

It's the new film. I keep telling them I look much better live . . . more vital. From now on I'm doing the shows right here at home. (*A pause.* ROGER *looks at* REBA *expectantly* ) Well?

REBA

Well what?

ROGER

Doesn't *anybody* notice anything?

(REBA *is puzzled.* ELLEN *looks at the set for the first time*)

ELLEN

Oh! Daddy's got a new toupee! (*She laughs uproariously*) I knew there was something funny.

REBA

(*Alarmed*)

Ellen! Stop that!

ROGER

(*With dignity*)

I fail to see what is so hilarious about a simple hair piece. For your information, John Cameron Swayze . . .

REBA

(*Placatingly*)

It's lovely, Roger, simply lovely. Your nicest one so far.

ROGER

(*A dark look at* ELLEN)

You don't think it's too much?

REBA

No. It's terribly romantic.

ROGER

(*Critically*)

The widow's peak all right?

REBA

(*A little shudder of excitement*)

Very becoming. So Latin!

ROGER

You don't think it makes me look too . . . sexy?

(ELLEN *is unable to stifle a giggle*)

REBA

Ellen!

ROGER

*(Defeated)*

I wish to hell I could hear what I'm saying.

(CONRAD *runs in from the porch, the green-looking zipper bag in one hand*)

CONRAD

*(Shouting)*

Hey, it's landing!

(ELLEN *gestures frantically at the bag, but* CONRAD *ignores her, dropping the bag on the armchair*)

ROGER

*What's* landing?

CONRAD

The spaceship.

(*He runs out onto the porch.* REBA *and* ROGER *follow*)

ROGER

As yet, there is no evidence to support such an hypothesis.

(ELLEN *hides the bag under the chair and runs after them. They look up at the sky; a light has begun to glow; a strange sound increases in volume*)

REBA

Why, look, Roger, something is coming this way. I hope it's not going to hit the house.

ROGER

The odds against being hit by a falling object that size are, I should say, roughly ten million to one.

CONRAD

It's not falling, it's *landing!*

ROGER

(*Losing control*)

Mass hysteria . . .

REBA

Shouldn't we go down to the cellar? Roger I'm frightened.

(*The white radiance now illuminates the whole portico.* ROGER *bolts inside just as the sound on the television set begins to work* )

ROGER

(*Terror*)

I'm going to call the police, the Army!

(*While the others watch outside, fascinated,* ROGER *telephones, his voice drowned by the booming telecast*)

TELEVISION VOICE

For several years now certain lunatic elements have proclaimed the existence of flying saucers. I should like to take this opportunity to nail the subject down once and for all: there jest ain't no sech animal: there is no life on other planets capable of building spaceships . . . and, to interject a purely American note, no country in the world but ours has the industrial know-how to build such a ship. . . .

(ROGER *returns excitedly to terrace, switching off set as he goes*)

ROGER

(*To set*)

Oh, shut up!

CONRAD

Here she comes.

ELLEN

Look how it shines!

REBA

Right in my rose garden!

(*An unearthly sound throbs from the garden*)

ROGER

General Powers is on his way over! He says we better leave the house.

CONRAD

Look! The whole side's opening.

(*The family start backing into the house*)

ELLEN

There's a man getting out!

REBA

Oh, I feel much better already. I'm sure if we ask him, he'll move that thing for us. Roger, you ask him.

(*A figure appears from the garden, silhouetted by the glare of light behind him*)

ROGER

(*Ominously*)

How do we know it's really a man? And not . . . not a monster?

(KRETON, *the visitor from outer space, enters.* KRETON *is a pleasant-looking man with side whiskers. He is dressed in the fashion of 1860. He approaches* ROGER)

KRETON

(*Politely*)

I hope the battle hasn't begun yet.

ROGER

Battle? There's no battle here.

KRETON

Oh, good. Then I'm in time. Please take me to General Robert E. Lee. I have a message for him.

ROGER

There isn't any General Lee staying here. There's just us, and General Powers, who's in Manassas. He's on a mission. Maybe you mean him.

(KRETON *notices* ROGER'S *suit. He looks at the others; then at himself. He realizes he is in the wrong century*)

KRETON

Oh, dear! I *am* sorry. I seem to've made a mistake. I'd better go back and start all over again.

(*He starts to the door, but* ROGER *stops him*)

ROGER

But you've only just arrived! Come in, come in. I don't need to tell you what a pleasure this is, Mister . . . Mister . . .

KRETON

Kreton. Off hand I should say I was about a hundred years out of my way.

ROGER

What?

KRETON

It's perfectly apparent. (*Points to the terrestrials*) Wrong costumes.

(*They look at their clothes*)

ROGER

Wrong for what?

KRETON

(*Indicates his own costume*)

I mean *I'm* in the wrong costume. For your century.

ROGER

Well, it is a bit old-fashioned.

REBA

But awfully handsome.

KRETON

Thank you.

REBA

(*Sotto voce*)

Roger, ask him to move that thing off the roses.

(ROGER *makes a hostly gesture*)

ROGER

Come on in, sir, and visit awhile. You must be tired after your trip.

KRETON

Yes, I am a bit.

ROGER

(*Indicates sofa*)

Sit right down here, sir.

(KRETON *sits on the sofa; the others regard him with wonder*)

KRETON

(*Looks about delightedly*)

Oh, it's even better than one imagined!

ROGER

Better? What's better?

KRETON

The "house" — that *is* what you call it? Or is this an "apartment"?

ROGER

It's a house all right.

KRETON

A real house! In the year — now, don't tell me — don't tell me because I know this period intimately: 1935 A.D.

ROGER

No, it's not 1935.

(KRETON *frowns, studies the room*)

KRETON

Not 1935 A.D.? Is that a "television" set over there?

ROGER

Yes.

KRETON

1965 A.D.

ROGER

You're getting warmer; it's 1957 and you're in the state of Virginia, U.S.A.

KRETON

(*Nods*)

Virginia, near Manassas. Right place, wrong year.

ELLEN

What year did you have in mind?

KRETON

1861 A.D. You see, I was on my way to the Battle of Bull Run when something went wrong with the machine and I landed here, a hundred years out of my way. (*Looks at Ellen thought-*

*fully*) But of course you're very nice too. Very nice. In fact, I shall give you a word of comfort: Hitler will not conquer the world. He will be exiled to an island in the Atantic.

ELLEN

Hitler's dead, Mr. Kreton. He killed himself.

CONRAD

And that was Napoleon on the island.

KRETON

Oh? So it was. You're perfectly right. But then I never was very good at dates, and of course, my poor head's rather a muddle after my trip. (*Sighs*) To think this is the twentieth century! I must collect myself. The real thing!

ELLEN

(*Tentatively*)

You . . . you aren't an American, are you?

KRETON

What a delightful idea! No, my dear, I'm not.

CONRAD

You sound more English.

KRETON

I suppose my accent must be frightful.

CONRAD

No, it's very good.

ROGER

Where *are* you from, Mr. Kreton?

KRETON

(*Pause*)

Another place.

ROGER

On this earth, of course.

KRETON

No, not on this planet.

ELLEN

Are you from Mars?

KRETON

Oh, dear, no! (*He roars with laughter at this absurdity* ) No one lives on Mars. At least no one *I* know!

ELLEN

I'm sure you're just teasing us and this is all some kind of wild publicity stunt.

ROGER

Incidentally, I'd certainly like to interview you on television while you're down here.

KRETON

I'm afraid your authorities won't permit it. They're frightfully upset as it is.

ROGER

How do you know?

KRETON

*(Evasively)*

Well, I . . . pick up things. For instance, I know that in a few minutes a number of people from your Army will be here to question me.

ROGER

Extraordinary!

ELLEN

Well, why did you come here?

KRETON

Oh, just a trip, a pleasure trip, a visit to your small planet. I've been studying you for ages. In fact, one might say you're a hobby of mine . . . especially this period of your development. (*He rises and recites happily* ) The planet Earth is the third planet of a 412 Sun K (and quite a nice sun it is!). Earth is divided into five continents with a number of large islands. It is mostly water. There is one . . . two? No, *one* moon. And at this particular moment civilization is just beginning.

ROGER

Just beginning? My dear sir . . .

KRETON

I only meant the initial stages of any civilization are always the most fascinating. I do hope I don't sound patronizing.

(*A siren is heard off stage* )

ELLEN

We're very proud. Especially in Virginia.

KRETON

That's one of your more endearing traits.

(GENERAL POWERS, *briefcase in hand, enters, accompanied by his youthful* AIDE, *an eager captain from West Point*)

POWERS

All right: the place is surrounded by troops. Where is the monster?

KRETON

I am the monster.

(POWERS *notices him for the first time*)

POWERS

You? Oh, no. (*Laughs scornfully*) What are you dressed up for?

KRETON

I had hoped to be in the right costume. But, unfortunately, I seem to've o'ershot my mark.

POWERS

Roger, who is this joker?

ROGER

(*Gabbling*)

This is Mr. Kreton . . . General Powers. Mr. Kreton arrived in that thing outside. He is from another planet.

POWERS

I don't believe it.

ELLEN

It's perfectly true. We saw him get out of the spaceship.

REBA

(*On familiar ground*)

Oh, Tom, this is little Ellen; you haven't seen her in years. Ellen, this is General Powers. (*To* POWERS) And this is Conrad Mayberry, a friend of Ellen's. He's staying for dinner too. (*To* CONRAD) You can stay, can't you?

(CONRAD *nods.* POWERS *has been trying to address the* AIDE *during this*)

POWERS

Captain, go down and look at that ship. But be careful. Don't touch anything. Don't let any of the men near. All right! (CAPTAIN *goes, and* POWERS *turns suspiciously to* KRETON ) So *you're* from another planet.

KRETON

Yes, indeed. (*Examining the general curiously*) That's a very smart uniform you're wearing, but I think I prefer the ones you used to wear, the ones with the feathers on top.

POWERS

All right, mister, there's one or two little matters I want cleared up.

KRETON

Certainly, General.

POWERS

Which planet you from?

KRETON

None you have ever heard of.

POWERS

Where is it?

KRETON

I couldn't begin to tell you.

POWERS

Is it in the solar system?

KRETON

No.

POWERS

In another system?

KRETON

More or less.

POWERS

Look, friend, let's not play twenty questions. I just want to know where you're from. The Pentagon requires it.

KRETON

But, my dear . . . "friend," it would take me years and years to teach you all you would need to know, and by the time I'd finished, you would be dead, because you *do* die, don't you?

POWERS

(*A new thought*)

Sooner or later, yes.

KRETON

(*Shudders*)

Such a disagreeable custom; poor fragile butterflies — a single brief moment in the sun, then: nothing. You see, we don't die.

POWERS

Well, you'll die if it turns out you're a spy or a hostile alien or something like that.

(AIDE *returns*)

AIDE

General Powers, sir.

POWERS

Well, what did you find?

AIDE

I don't know, sir.

POWERS

(*Heavy irony*)

Then will you kindly do your West Point best to describe what the object in question is like?

AIDE

Well, it's an oblate spheroid with a fourteen-foot diameter and it's made of an unknown metal which shines all over and inside there isn't anything, no instruments, no food, nothing.

(*He salutes and marches off*)

POWERS

(*Bewildered*)

What did you do with your instrument board?

KRETON

With my what? Oh, I don't have one.

POWERS

Well, how does that thing travel?

KRETON

Honestly, I don't know. It just goes.

POWERS

Now, look, mister, you're in pretty serious trouble and I suggest you do a bit of cooperating. You don't expect us to believe that that contraption travels around through outer space with no instruments.

KRETON

Of course it does. We all travel this way. I suppose once upon a time I must've known how these little cars operate, but I've quite forgotten. After all, General, we're not mechanics, you and I. We mustn't clutter our minds with trivia. It just gets me there and it gets me back.

(REBA *turns to* ROGER *and whispers hoarsely*)

REBA

I'll go make up the guest room.

(*She goes upstairs.* POWERS *turns to* ROGER)

POWERS

Can we use your study, Roger?

ROGER

By all means.

KRETON

"Use your study": how beguiling! And *what* will we use it for?

(POWERS *gestures for* KRETON *to precede him into the study.* KRETON, *with a glad smile at the family, does so. As* KRETON *and* POWERS *enter the study,* ROGER *rushes out onto portico*)

ROGER

I'm going down to look at the ship.

(CONRAD *and* ELLEN *follow, but not before* ELLEN, *exasperated, indicates the green-looking zipper bag. In the study,* POWERS *girds for the moment of truth* )

POWERS

Are you deliberately trying to confuse me?

KRETON

Oh, my, no . . . not deliberately.

POWERS

You tell me you are not from this world, yet you don't actually live on any other planet. It's double talk.

KRETON

In a sense, I suppose we *do* live on a planet; though actually we don't — if you see what I mean.

POWERS

No, I do not.

KRETON

We live — now let me see; you have a crude word for it. Keep on thinking; that's right. Oh, there it is, bobbing around in your mind: *dimension*. We live in another dimension, in the suburbs of time, you might say.

POWERS

The what?

KRETON

The suburbs of time. A happy phrase.

POWERS

All right. All right. Now the Pentagon requires one or two forms to be filled out. (*He sits at his desk, opens his briefcase, removing a stack of forms and rubber stamps* ) Now, let's start from the beginning. You say you've come here as a tourist?

KRETON

Yes (POWERS *eagerly stamps forms in quadruplicate*), you might say I'm a tourist.

POWERS

(*Sitting back*)

Mr. Kreton, I think I should tell you that it is my job to guard the security of this country.

KRETON

What interesting work!

POWERS

And, frankly, I think that you are a spy sent here by an alien race to study us, preparatory to invasion.

KRETON

(*Reveling in this*)

Delicious! Would you say that again — I loved it.

POWERS

No, I will not say it again. And I suggest you get down to brass tacks, mister. If your people are thinking of invasion, they should know that we're ready for them. (*Rising heroically*) We'll fight them with everything we've got. We'll fight them with the hydrogen bomb, with poison gas, with broken beer bottles if necessary; we'll fight them on the beaches; we'll fight them in the alleys; we'll fight them . . .

KRETON

Oh, General, that's splendid! Really splendid! Look, I'm covered with gooseflesh just listening to you.

POWERS

I wasn't finished.

KRETON

I know. However, I should tell you that my people would never dream of invading you.

POWERS

How do I know that's true?

KRETON

You don't, and like so many other things down here, you must take it on faith. For instance, I must warn you that I can tell what's inside.

POWERS

What's inside what?

KRETON

Your mind.

POWERS

(*Disbelief*)

You're a mind reader?

KRETON

Well, I don't exactly read it. I hear it.

POWERS

(*Complacently*)

All right, what am I thinking?

(KRETON *listens a moment. We hear a martial mind-wave*)

KRETON

If this joker's not a lunatic, he's a Communist spy.

POWERS

You could've guessed that. (*Pause*) All right, *now* what am I thinking?

KRETON

How amusing! How *very amusing.* (*There is a long pause*

*while* KRETON *listens to the general's thoughts with obvious delight* ) Who *is* Lieutenant General Son-of-a-bitch Claypoole?

POWERS
(*Stricken*)

My God!

KRETON

*And* Major General Spotty McClelland? (GENERAL POWERS *sinks weakly into a chair*) You feel persecuted. You believe these two gentlemen plan to wreck your career.

POWERS

Believe! I *know!*

KRETON

You also think that if you can "handle" me, your promotion will be secured. I must say I think you're a bit optimistic about your career, but believe me, anything I can do to help, I will. I like you, General.

POWERS
(*Touched*)

That's very decent of you. I mean (*Pulls himself together, returns to his forms*) I'm glad you see the wisdom of cooperating. Very well: (a) Are you the first of your race to visit the earth?

KRETON

Oh, I should think so, and even this little visit of mine smacks of the impromptu. I'm a creature of impulse, I fear!

POWERS

(*Stamps appropriate forms*)

(b) Are there apt to be any more of you arriving in the near future?

KRETON

Goodness, no! No one would ever dream of visiting *you!* Except me. But then, of course, I'm a hobbyist. I love to gad about.

(*Telephone on the desk rings.* POWERS *answers it*)

POWERS

(*Into phone*)

Yes, yes, this is General Powers speaking. Oh, the Chief of Staff. Certainly. Put him right on. (*His face lights up with sycophantic zeal* ) Hello? Yes, sir, Powers speaking. Yes, sir, I'm talking to him right now. . . . No, sir. . . . No, sir. We haven't been able to determine what method of power was used, but we're working on it. . . . No, he won't talk. . . . What? (*He looks at* KRETON *thoughtfully* ) Well, he *looks* human. Just a minute, I'll ask him. (*To* KRETON) Mr. Kreton, are you a mammal?

KRETON

For all practical purposes.

POWERS

He *says* he's a mammal. . . . Yes, sir. I'll hold him here. I've put the house under martial law . . . Who? Oh, yes, sir. I realize the importance of it. Yes, I will. Good-by. (*He hangs up and turns with quiet dignity to* KRETON) The President of the United States wants to know all about you.

KRETON

How very nice! And I shall want to know all about him. Coolidge, isn't it?

POWERS

No, it is not Coolidge.

KRETON

Ah, well. You have so many of them. Tell him I'll see him tomorrow. Now I should really like to rest.

POWERS

Well, while you're resting, we'll take your ship apart.

KRETON

Oh, now, you mustn't do that!

POWERS

Sorry. Security demands it.

KRETON

Well, I'm awfully afraid *my* security demands you leave it alone.

POWERS

Look, Buster, you're under martial law. You can't stop us. Nobody can. Order Secretary Defense.

KRETON

*(Gestures)*

I hate to be a spoilsport, but . . . !

*(Muffled cries from beyond the porch. The* AIDE *appears from the garden, rushes into the study)*

AIDE

*(Frightened)*

Something's happened to the ship! The door's shut and there's some kind of wall all around it . . . an invisible wall. We can't get near it!

KRETON

I hope there was no one inside.

POWERS

*(Stunned)*

How did you do that?

KRETON

I don't think I could *ever* explain it to you.

(POWERS *backs away apprehensively*)

POWERS

You're making us look damned silly, you realize that? *(He backs into the* AIDE; *this recalls him to duty. He looks at the* AIDE, *then at* KRETON ) Can you tell what *he's* thinking?

KRETON

Of course. Would you care to listen?

POWERS

Yes.

(KRETON *gestures. The* AIDE'*s mind fills the room*)

AIDE'S MIND

Well, it sure looks like old Lead-Ass has got his hands full this time.

(KRETON *gestures again, and the* AIDE'*s mind goes off abruptly.* POWERS, *poleaxed, regards the trembling* AIDE *stolidly*)

POWERS

(*Gently martyred*)

You may go, Captain!

(AIDE *salutes, about-faces, then runs off stage to the garden*)

KRETON

Old Lead-Ass! What an enchanting figure of speech!

POWERS

One of Claypoole's people! They're everywhere.

(ROGER *enters the living room. He starts to make a telephone call, thinks better of it, picks up a telephone book, starts to hall*)

KRETON

Our hosts are approaching. Do let's join them. It's greedy of me, keeping you all to myself, General.

(POWERS, *followed by* KRETON, *goes into the living room.* ROGER *surreptitiously sneaks past them upstairs* )

POWERS

*(Mumbling)*

Treachery . . . treachery. . . . My own aide.

*(Continues on to terrace and off stage as* CONRAD *and* ELLEN *enter)*

KRETON

Did you have a nice look-see?

CONRAD

Very, until you blocked us.

KRETON

Ah, well, I couldn't allow them to wreck my poor little car. *(He sits down, suddenly delighted )* You know, I can hardly believe you're real!

CONRAD

I guess we're all in the same boat.

KRETON

All in the same . . . ? Oh, yes. A metaphor! How nice! I do hope I haven't upset things too much, arriving like this.

ELLEN

Oh, we love it!

CONRAD

Just how long did it take you to get here?

KRETON

The better part of a day.

CONRAD

One day?

KRETON

One of our days, but then you don't know about time yet.

CONRAD

You mean relativity.

KRETON

Oh, it's more involved than that. You see, you won't know about time until — now let me think a minute . . . (*Looks about*) You have electricity. Those aren't gaslights, are they?

CONRAD

Oh, no. We've got electricity and atomic power and hydrogen bombs . . .

KRETON

Isn't hydrogen fun! Anyway, you won't learn about time for ages and ages. . . . You know, I was rather put out at first, arriving at the . . . the wrong address, but now I think I'm going to have a really nice visit.

ELLEN

Well, I hope we won't be too dull for you, after traveling in space and everything.

KRETON

Oh, quite the contrary. As a matter of fact, I've just had a delicious idea — something so simple, yet so . . . But here I am chattering about me, when I want to hear all about *you!*

CONRAD

But you know all about us. And we don't know anything about you. For instance, what were you going to do back in 1861?

KRETON

Observe your Civil War. I dote on the Civil War.

CONRAD

And you can actually travel through time?

KRETON

Oh, yes! Time and space are the same thing, you know.

(GENERAL POWERS *enters from the porch. The* AIDE *takes up guard duty at the door. As* POWERS *crosses gloomily to hall,* KRETON *speaks*)

KRETON

It won't work, General.

POWERS

What won't work?

KRETON

Destroying my force field with a hydrogen bomb. You'll simply wreak havoc amongst Mrs. Spelding's roses.

(POWERS *glares and marches out through the hall*)

ELLEN

(*Intrigued*)

Can you tell what we're all thinking?

KRETON

Ah, yes. As a matter of fact, it makes me rather giddy. You see, your minds are not at all like ours: we control our thoughts, while you . . . well, it's extraordinary the way your thoughts simply tumble about!

ELLEN

Can you tell *everything* we think?

KRETON

Everything! (*He listens a moment* ) I *am* sorry to have interrupted your trip to Richmond. But don't let me keep you. The Claude Ollingers are expected at Cottage D . . .

CONRAD

I'll be damned.

ROGER

(*From off stage*)

Powers!

ELLEN

Don't tell Daddy.

(ROGER *comes down in a rage*)

ROGER

Powers! Where are you, Powers?

(POWERS *enters from hall door*)

POWERS

Yes, Roger?

ROGER

I am unable to make a telephone call in my own house. A guard at the front door tells me I cannot leave without *your* permission. Powers, the Constitution still stands.

POWERS

Now, now, Roger, until I've received word from Washington as to the final disposition of this . . . problem, you will have to obey my orders. No telephone calls. No communication with the outside. No one can leave this house till further notice.

ELLEN

(*Alarmed*)

But Conrad and I are going to Richmond . . . to the *movies.* Aren't we, Conrad?

CONRAD

That's right. And we better get started. The feature goes on at . . .

ROGER

(*Disgust*)

At a time like this, Conrad goes to the movies.

(CONRAD *and* ELLEN *start out terrace door*)

POWERS

Don't move, and that's an order.

CONRAD

(*To* POWERS)

I've *got* to stay here?

POWERS

Anybody who knows about this joker must remain under military surveillance. If word leaked out now, there'd be an international panic.

ROGER

I am a member of the free press . . .

POWERS

You'll be allowed to do your regular broadcast. But no mention of . . . (*He points toward* KRETON ) Savvy?

(REBA *enters from the hall*)

CONRAD

(*To* POWERS)

Look, I *can't* stay. I'd like to, of course, but I've got this poor goat . . .

(REBA *unerringly discovers the green bag. She picks it up*)

REBA

(*To* CONRAD)

Is that your bag?

CONRAD

Yes, it is.

ELLEN

(*Quickly*)

He's going to spend the night. General Powers says he has to.

REBA

I wish you'd given me a little more notice. We've got only the one guest room and Mr. Kreton's using that. . . . Well, all right. I can move in with Ellen, and Conrad can sleep with you, Roger.

ROGER

Oh, now, damn it . . .

KRETON

(*Interrupting*)

Poor Mr. Spelding; I *am* upsetting things. Shall I leave? I think it would solve everything.

ROGER

(*Furious*)

Yes! (*Then he sees* POWERS *signaling "no" behind* KRETON'S *back* ) You must stay. I mean, got to be hospitable, want you to get a good impression of us . . .

KRETON

Then I shall remain.

(*Turns and smiles at* POWERS)

POWERS

Thank you.

KRETON

Don't mention it.

ROGER

I wonder, Mr. Kreton, if I may ask you a few questions. You know, off the record, background stuff . . .

KRETON

By all means, off the record!

ROGER

Now, you know I like to level with people and, well, we're afraid you belong to a . . . to a hostile race.

KRETON

And I've assured General Powers that my people are not remotely predatory. In fact, except for me, no one is interested in you. Oh, dear, I shouldn't have said that! Anyway, *I* adore you and that's all that matters. *You are my hobby*. I love you.

POWERS

(*Heavily*)

That's certainly decent of you.

ROGER

So you've come down here for an on-the-spot visit, sort of going native.

KRETON

What a nice turn of phrase. Exactly. I am going native.

POWERS

Well, it is my view that you have been sent here by another civilization for the express purpose of reconnoitering prior to invasion.

KRETON

That would be your view! The wonderfully primitive assumption that all strangers are hostile. Oh, General, you're almost too good to be true.

POWERS

You deny your people intend to make trouble for us?

KRETON

I deny it.

ROGER

Well, then are they, ah, interested in establishing trade, communications?

KRETON

But we've always had communication. And as for trade, well, we just do not trade; it's an activity peculiar to *your* social level. (*Quickly*) Which I'm not criticizing, mind you! I love all the things you do!

ROGER

In any case, you have no plans to, well, to dominate the earth. We have your solemn assurance of that.

KRETON

(*Blandly*)

No. I'm sorry, but you haven't.

(*The terrestrials respond with alarm*)

ROGER

We haven't? I thought you said your people weren't interested in conquest.

KRETON

They're not, but *I* am.

POWERS

You?

KRETON

Me — I mean *I*. . . . I have decided to take charge.

POWERS

Of the United States?

KRETON

Oh, no, everything, the whole world. All of it. All mine.

ROGER

That's insane!

POWERS

Cockeyed! How can one man take over the world?

KRETON

(*Diffidently*)

I admit I'm leaping into this on the spur of the moment, but . . .

POWERS

(*To* AIDE)

Grab him! (POWERS, CAPTAIN *and* CONRAD *rush* KRETON, *but within a foot of him they stop, blocked by an invisible wall* ) You are under arrest.

KRETON

(*Laughs*)

You can't touch me. I should've warned you. That's part of the game. Oh, we're going to have such good times!

(*All stare with horror at* KRETON *except* REBA, *who has been thinking ahead*)

REBA

Now, since there're so many of us, I thought we'd have a buffet supper. Everything's set up in the dining room. (*To* KRETON) You'll have supper with us, won't you? I'm afraid it's not very elaborate. You see, we didn't know . . .

KRETON

You're very good, but if you don't mind, I'd prefer a little lie-down. I'm a bit tired.

REBA

I'll show you your room.

KRETON

Don't bother. I know the way. (*Touches his brow*) Such savage thoughts! My head is vibrating like a drum. I feel quite odd, all of you thinking at once.

(*He gestures and we hear, in order*)

ROGER'S MIND

I realize, ladies and gentlemen, that the Nobel Prize you have just given me . . .

REBA'S MIND

Since Mr. Kreton isn't eating, that leaves just enough chicken for everybody . . .

CONRAD'S MIND

Ellen, honey, I'm here. Right here in the house . . . (*Then, sadly*) with *Daddy.*

ELLEN'S MIND

This is all a dream. It's been a hot, muggy day and I've fallen asleep in the swing.

POWERS' MIND

This joker can't take over the world. Napoleon couldn't. Hitler couldn't. I can't.

(*Then* KRETON *gestures. All the minds are heard at once; a terrible babble*)

KRETON

You see? Quite overpowering. And so good night, children, dear *wicked* children. Tomorrow will be a wonderful day for all of us. Sleep tight!

(*He goes upstairs with a flourish*)

CURTAIN

# ACT TWO

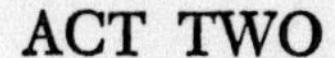

## Scene One

## ACT TWO

### Scene One

*It is the next morning.*

*The aide sits with an army carbine across his knees on the porch. He is dozing fitfully.*

*Kreton is in the living room, wearing a handsome brocaded dressing gown of the sort one associates with Prince Albert. He holds a cat to whom he talks genially and without condescension.*

KRETON

And they live in here? But where? I can't see a thing. Oh, down there! (*He crosses to the wall and examines a small hole at floor level* ) You say there are a great many of them *inside* the wall? How very interesting! No, no. I'm not hungry, but I agree it would be great fun to hunt together. Oh, come now, you're just flattering me. I'm sure I'd make an awful botch of it! Well, I suppose I *could* leap, but I wouldn't be fast enough and, of course, I haven't your lovely sharp teeth. . . . No, I don't suppose mice are very clever, but then they lead such awfully common lives. . . . I'm sure they must be delicious to eat! Ugh! Oh, of course if I meet any, I'll let you know. (*He stretches out on the sofa, cat in hand* ) Oh, dear, no! Don't tell me! I do sympathize with you: dogs *are* distasteful. What? Oh, I can well believe they are. . . . Yes, yes, how disgusting! They don't even groom their fur? But you do, constantly; such a fine coat. No, no, I'm not just saying that. I really mean it. Exquisite texture. . . . What? They chase you? Dogs chase you out of malice? Poor little creature! But then you do fight back. . . . That's right. You let them have it! Slash, bite, scratch! Don't let them off easy! Rip their eyes out! How gloriously savage! What? Oh, no, no, no, I wouldn't dare. People would complain if I were to shoot their dogs. Eh? I could run over them with a car? Make it look like an accident? Oh, you are fiendishly clever.

(ELLEN *enters from the hall, carrying a breakfast tray*)

ELLEN

Good morning.

KRETON

Good morning.

ELLEN

I brought you your breakfast.

KRETON

That's very thoughtful of you, but, alas, I do not eat.

ELLEN

You don't eat anything at all?

KRETON

No. Nothing. Different metabolic system. (*Examines tray with delight*) An authentic mid-twentieth-century breakfast! I've seen them in museums, of course, but never so horribly real. (*Prods food with a fork, a look of horror and wonder on his face*) This was *torn* from some animal, wasn't it?

ELLEN

Oh, no, that's bacon.

KRETON

But it was connected with an animal at one time.

ELLEN

Why, yes, of course it was . . . how silly of me! Bacon comes from a pig.

KRETON

(*Turns to the cat*)

What did you say? Of course you can have it. No, no, it's quite all right. I'm not a bit hungry.

(*He gives the cat the bacon*)

ELLEN

(*Wide-eyed*)

Were you *talking* to Rosemary?

KRETON

Oh, yes. We've had such a nice chat . . . all about dogs and mice.

ELLEN

You can see inside her mind, too?

KRETON

(*Nods*)

Oh, yes . . . exactly the same principle. Same raw, blazing emotions . . . though somewhat one-track. Not unlike General Powers, actually.

ELLEN

Does Rosemary like us?

KRETON

No, I'm afraid Rosemary doesn't.

ELLEN

I don't believe you. Here, Rosemary, here, kitty.

(*She reaches for the cat, who retreats as all proper cats do when menaced by affection*)

KRETON

Her mind is now aflame with revulsion.

ELLEN

Well, she's really Mother's pet. . . . Beast!

KRETON

Oh, I can't begin to tell you how wonderful it is being here! And not at all the way I thought.

ELLEN

Why? What did you imagine?

KRETON

Well, you know how one feels about history, the glamour of the past; I expected to hear everybody talking about great events — battles, poets, that kind of thing — but of course you don't. You just squabble among yourselves.

ELLEN

We don't squabble *all* the time. And you keep talking about us being in the past. Are you from the future?

KRETON

In a way, yes. You see, time is really all the same thing and I am in a position where I can visit you at any moment in your history. Time is a trapezoid.

ELLEN

(*At sea*)

I'm not awfully good at science. You see, I'm majoring in art appreciation.

KRETON

I'm sure you must be very . . . appreciative.

ELLEN

Do you do a lot of traveling in space?

KRETON

A goodish bit.

ELLEN

What's it like in space?

KRETON

Drab. But it can be quite nice in season. (*Listens to cat*) I'll ask her. (*To* ELLEN) She wants to know if she can have the other piece of bacon.

ELLEN

No. Bacon's bad for her. Besides, she doesn't like us.

KRETON

I don't think she'll grasp the subtlety of *that.* (*Pause*) No, she has not grasped it. . . . Oh, no! Rosemary, you are awful!

ELLEN

What did she say?

KRETON

I wouldn't dare repeat it. Besides, it would lose too much in translation!

ELLEN

Nasty animal. Go away!

(*Takes the cat into hall*)

KRETON

Where is your family? I haven't seen anyone today except you and the cat.

ELLEN

Father went to Washington with General Powers. Mother got permission to go shopping, and poor Conrad's still asleep.

KRETON

Oh, yes! Poor Conrad! Now, my girl, out with it. Tell me everything.

ELLEN

Everything about what?

KRETON

There is no use in being evasive.

(*Gestures*)

ELLEN'S MIND

It's all such a mess. Poor Conrad's sleeping with Daddy and wearing Daddy's pajamas because there wasn't anything in that green zipper bag except some old telephone books which Mr. and Mrs. Claude Ollinger *always* take with them when they travel. Well, maybe this afternoon when Mr. Kreton leaves, *if* he leaves — oh, he's inside! Mr. Kreton's inside my mind. Stop that, Mr. Kreton!

ELLEN

Stop that, Mr. Kreton!

ELLEN'S MIND

A girl's got to have some privacy.

ELLEN

A girl's got to have some privacy.

ELLEN'S MIND

I'm saying everything I think.

ELLEN

I'm saying everything I think.

ELLEN'S MIND

This is awful! Please stop.

ELLEN

This is awful! Please stop.

KRETON

(*Gestures*)

I didn't want to embarrass you, but you mustn't keep things from me. It's impossible.

ELLEN

Well, now you know. The whole thing's so mixed up.

KRETON

Then shall we unmix it? Offhand, I should say your problem, essentially, is one of housing. Conrad must stay here. So far so good. *But,* unhappily for your purposes, he has elected to sleep in your father's room.

ELLEN

No, he didn't. He doesn't like Daddy.

KRETON

Then am I to understand that it was your father who insisted on this arrangement?

ELLEN

Oh, no! Daddy despises Conrad.

KRETON

It is complex. But *not* unsolvable. Now: There are three bedrooms. I occupy one. The four of you must occupy the other two, in pairs. Threes, I gather, are taboo. Very well. Let us be logical. Methodical. Two must go into Room A. And two into Room B.

Since the present combination is unsatisfactory, I propose — now listen closely — that Mr. and Mrs. Spelding *together* occupy Room A while you and Conrad — oh, this is brilliant! — occupy Room B.

ELLEN

But Conrad and I aren't married.

KRETON

Neither were Mr. and Mrs. Claude Ollinger.

ELLEN

(*Flustered*)

Well, that was different.

KRETON

Not in the least. You had planned to devote all of last night to wild abandon, you and Conrad and the four telephone books. How glorious you must be! Tangled in one another's arms, looking up telephone numbers. . . . I suppose that's what you *were* planning to do with those books. So bizarre, the whole thing.

ELLEN

You're going to make me blush, Mr. Kreton.

KRETON

Forgive me . . . but I find the whole subject fascinating because, you see, where I come from, we do not tangle.

ELLEN

You don't!

KRETON

No, not for a very long time. We gave it up, along with the appendix and the fifth toe.

ELLEN

But what do you do?

KRETON

Well, we do a lot of reading and gadding about, here and there, one thing and another. Oh, we keep busy.

ELLEN

But how . . . how do you multiply?

KRETON

Multiply what?

ELLEN

Each other. How do you have babies?

KRETON

We don't.

ELLEN

I don't understand.

KRETON

Well, you see, we have ourselves, and since we don't die, we don't need any more of us! So we gave it up. . . . I sometimes wonder if we weren't rather hasty. (*Briskly*) Anyway, you must promise to let me watch the next time you make love. It's one of the things I *most* want to see while I'm down here. I should particularly like to watch you with some strapping boy — Conrad if you like, except he's not awake yet; or perhaps we can use that young captain on the porch. (*Crosses to porch door*) I'm sure he hasn't anything better to do. Come along now and let's get started. Captain! Oh, Captain!

(*The* AIDE *comes to alert attention*)

ELLEN

(*Horrified*)

Why, that's disgusting!

KRETON

(*Bewildered*)

Oh? But . . . but it's on your minds so much I simply assumed it was all quite public. I *am* sorry if I've put my foot in it. All right, Captain. You're excused.

(*The* AIDE *returns to his post*)

ELLEN

Of course I know you're from another planet and all and I guess we do *think* an awful lot about sex, but we're not supposed to talk about it and we only do it when nobody's looking.

KRETON

How ravishing! These primitive taboos. You revel in public slaughter: you pay to watch two men hit one another repeatedly, yet you make love secretly, guiltily and with remorse . . . too delicious!

ELLEN

You sound awfully superior.

KRETON

(*Quiet pride*)

We are. But it was not easy. It took us ages to stamp out disease — scarlet fever, mumps, anxiety, the common cold and, finally, the great killer itself, the ultimate disease: passion!

ELLEN

Passion?

KRETON

Love, hate, that kind of thing. Passion — the Hydra-headed monster, so difficult to diagnose: love-nest slayings, bad temper, world wars, verse tragedies in five acts — so many variants. But at last success crowned our efforts. And now . . . we feel nothing. We do nothing. We are perfect.

ELLEN

That sounds terribly dull!

KRETON

How neatly you put it. And that's why I'm here. To escape the dreary company of Delton 4.

ELLEN

Delton 4?

KRETON

Yes, he's the most niggling. Though Deltons 1, 2 and 3 are hardly prize packages. In fact, I am afraid that in our perfection we have become intergalactic bores. Our continuum is rather a frost. (CONRAD *enters sleepily, from upstairs* ) Good morning, Conrad. Did you sleep well?

CONRAD

No. I was up all night. Ellen, your father grinds his teeth. It's just gruesome.

(*He sinks onto the sofa*)

ELLEN

He's been reading my mind . . .

KRETON

And I know everything! All about the madcap Ollingers looking up telephone numbers . . .

CONRAD

Doing what?

ELLEN

(*Apologetically*)

I couldn't help it. He saw it in my mind.

(*They embrace.* KRETON *watches discreetly*)

KRETON

*Heard* it, actually. Such a confused mind, no concentration.

ELLEN

(*Suddenly alert*)

I may be confused, but I have enormous powers of concentration. Just you watch. All right, Conrad, pick a book — either book.

(CONRAD *selects a book from the table* — The Judgment of Paris *by Gore Vidal, an odd coincidence — she opens it and studies the first page a moment*)

CONRAD

This is absolutely the most pointless trick.

KRETON

What is she going to do — tear it in half?

CONRAD

Hey, now *that* would be a stunt! She's got very strong wrists and maybe with a little practice . . .

(ELLEN *hands the open book to* KRETON; *then with a demure, complacent smile she begins to recite in a flat, uninflected voice*)

ELLEN

"Chapter One. She wore her trauma like a plume. When she was seven an elderly man attempted to have his way with her in a telephone booth at Grand Central Station (her mother had been buying a ticket to Peekskill). Although in no way defiled, the shock was great and, to this day, she was so terrified of the telephone that . . ."

CONRAD

O.K., honey. O.K.

KRETON

(*Enmeshed*)

How very lurid! And once again the telephone motif, the hidden symbol . . .

ELLEN

It's sort of lush, isn't it? Well, what do you think?

(KRETON *is thumbing the pages eagerly*)

KRETON

Starts nicely, but I'd have to read a little more to tell.

ELLEN

No, I meant about my concentration. I can do the whole page. (*She starts again*) ". . . so terrified of the telephone that . . ."

CONRAD

(*Quickly*)

She can. Don't dispute her.

KRETON

I shan't and I agree: it *is* impressive. For a lower primate, quite good. Rather the way we do things.

ELLEN

Then show me how.

KRETON

How what?

ELLEN

How you do things . . . you know, like hear minds and travel around the universe.

KRETON

But you haven't the concentration. I mean, what you do is very good, of course, but you see, we use a hundred per cent of the mind, while you, dear creature, use about five per cent.

CONRAD

And sometimes less.

KRETON

And sometimes less.

ELLEN

Show me anyway.

KRETON

How stubborn you are. A will of iron. Very well. A simple demonstration. Now watch this.

(*With a flourish, he points, and a vase on the mantelpiece rises a foot in the air and then returns to its place*)

CONRAD

(*Queasy*)

Oh, no. Don't do that.

KRETON

See? I lifted the vase with my mind. I *thought* it into the air. Couldn't be simpler.

ELLEN

Now let me try. What do I do?

(*Eagerly she crosses to* KRETON)

KRETON

Really, it's quite hopeless! Well, if it amuses you . . . shut your eyes. . . . That's right. Now focus all your thoughts on that vase. (ELLEN *frowns intently* ) Well, go on. Lift it.

(*She makes a great effort, jerking her head*)

ELLEN

(*Finally*)

Nothing happened.

KRETON

Because as usual you were thinking of a dozen things at once: love-making with Conrad, your father's intransigence, my plans for the world . . .

ELLEN

Let me try again . . . just one more time.

CONRAD

She's sort of a pest.

KRETON

Sort of a monomaniac. Very well then. Shut your eyes. Empty your dear tiny mind. Ready . . . set . . . go! Lift the vase, lift the vase, lift the vase . . .

(*He repeats this over and over.* ELLEN, *her face contorted, her body rigid, concentrates. At last, to* CONRAD'S *horror, the vase rises an inch, then drops back on the mantel with a sharp noise*)

CONRAD

Oh, no!

ELLEN

It moved! It moved! It really moved!

KRETON

How very clever! I must say I never thought you could do it.

CONRAD

(*Alarmed*)

You helped her, didn't you?

KRETON

No, she did it all by herself. Oh, my dear, what a success you'll be at parties.

ELLEN

(*Empire-building*)

Now I've done that, show me how you hear minds.

KRETON

No, I think that's quite enough for now.

(REBA *enters from porch with groceries. A bleak military policeman who has been following her takes up his post at the door*)

KRETON

Ah, Mrs. Spelding, and have we had a nice morning?

REBA

(*Furious*)

Nice! It's been horrible, simply horrible! Everywhere I went a soldier went with me. And how could I explain him? I mean, people would come up and say, "Hello, Reba, how are you?" And I'd start to tell them and he'd shut me up with a gun! With a gun! Oh, I know it's fun for you men, Mr. Kreton, but I'm the laughingstock of Manassas with a gun literally held to my temple in the Piggly Wiggly!

(*Marches off into the hall*)

KRETON

I do seem to be causing a disturbance.

ELLEN

Well, we love it. Oh, it's such fun having you here!

KRETON

(*Touched*)

Dear children . . .

ELLEN

But one thing . . . you . . . you weren't serious, were you? What you said last night about taking charge of the world?

KRETON

Of course I was serious!

ELLEN

I told Daddy I thought you were joking.

KRETON

Well, I wasn't. I'll admit the idea didn't occur to me until General Powers suggested it with his bellicose thoughts.

CONRAD

How do you plan to do this . . . taking over?

KRETON

I hate to admit it, but I haven't quite decided.

ELLEN

But why *do* you want to take over the world?

KRETON

Oh, I have a project or two . . . this and that. (*Laughs*) It'll be great fun.

CONRAD

No, it won't. You'd hate it. You'd have to make speeches every day and shake hands and lay cornerstones . . . and all that paper work.

KRETON

(*Frowns*)

Well, I agree I shouldn't like to be cooped up in an office. But then why couldn't I take charge secretly?

ELLEN

How would you do that?

KRETON

(*Nettled*)

I wish you'd stop asking me how I plan to do things when I don't even know myself.

ELLEN

Well! It's awfully interesting. And anyway, if someone goes around saying he wants to take charge of the world, he should at least think it through first.

KRETON

You sound exactly like Delton 4. It's not my fault I'm impulsive — heart rules the head and all that. . . . Very well then, let's give it some thought. If you're so clever, you can help me think of something.

(*All three frown thoughtfully and, in a circle, pace around the living room.* CONRAD *stops suddenly in front of the mantelpiece. He points at the vase*)

CONRAD

Couple of tricks like raising that thing over there would just about do it.

KRETON

Oh, yes, parlor tricks! Of course. Alarm the natives. Great White Father and all that! Yes, I *could* dry up one of the smaller oceans.

CONRAD

Oh, no!

KRETON

A bit much? Overalarm them?

ELLEN

Yes.

CONRAD

It overalarms me.

KRETON

Or I could do something odd to the moon. (*He looks at the alarmed couple* ) No, you're both looking a bit panicky and of course I want you to behave naturally. That's why I'm here. To see you as you are, not as I might make you be.

CONRAD

I think it would be a mistake to start monkeying around with the moon.

KRETON

You're absolutely right. *Subtlety* is called for. I must remain in the background. A gray eminence. Pulling the strings.

ELLEN

But how?

KRETON

(*Sharply*)

Will you stop rushing me? I told you I'm just improvising. . . . All right now! Here's a smasher, but not a word to anyone. It must be our secret. Only the three of us will know. (*He starts to gesture, then he stops with an embarrassed giggle* ) Oh, dear, I do hope I'm not descending to the level of the cheaply theatrical. . . . Well (*Gestures*), here goes!

(*On the porch the* AIDE*'s rifle leaps from his hands and rises to the proscenium.* KRETON, ELLEN *and* CONRAD *run out onto the porch*)

AIDE

(*Hysterical*)

My gun . . . my gun . . . it just jumped out of my hands.

KRETON

Jumped out of your hands! Too alarming! Now, I wonder how that could've happened? (*Winks at* CONRAD *and* ELLEN) How very sinister!

AIDE

I was just holding it. . . . Oh, I'll be court-martialed. General Powers is just waiting for something like this to happen. Just because I went to West Point and he didn't. And I was in Claypoole's office for two lousy weeks, so he thinks I'm a spy. And then that awful thing he heard me thinking last night . . .

(*Sinks onto bench*)

KRETON

Now, don't take on so. I'll intercede for you. Besides, whatever goes up, quite frequently comes down.

(*He leads* CONRAD *and* ELLEN *back inside. The* AIDE *continues to stare miserably at the rifle*)

KRETON

Well?

ELLEN

I hope he won't be in any trouble.

KRETON

Unlikely. Since all the rifles in all the world are now floating through the air some fifteen feet off the ground.

CONRAD

All of them?

KRETON

All of them. (*Gestures. The rifle falls and the* AIDE *catches it with a shout* ) And now they have them back.

CONRAD

You know, every time you do something like that I get this kind of sick feeling, right here. Not that it isn't exciting and so on, but . . .

(GENERAL POWERS, *a prince of gloom, enters from the hall, briefcase in hand*)

POWERS

Well, good morning, Mr. Kreton, and how are we today?

KRETON

Absolutely wallowing in the twentieth century.

POWERS

Oh? Well, I don't need to say that there's been quite a bit of excitement at the Pentagon and . . . (*Turns to* CONRAD *and* ELLEN) I'm afraid this is top secret.

CONRAD

Come on, honey.

KRETON

Forgive me, children . . . but remember . . . our little top secret.

ELLEN

We won't breathe a word.

(CONRAD *and* ELLEN *run off through the porch door*)

POWERS

Well, Mr. Kreton, they have won . . . again.

KRETON

Who won what?

POWERS

I put it up to you, Mr. Kreton, as an impartial observer — I assume you're impartial — why should *I* be the one who has to carry the ball on this project: Operation Kreton? Not that I haven't enjoyed knowing you — I mean, that's one of the great things about Army life; you get to meet all kinds of people, from different places, or, in this case, different *planets* — but after all, Interserv. Strat. Tac.'s mission is a larger one, covering, as you know, saddle making, dry cleaning, hygiene and, of course, laundry. So why, I asked the Chief of Staff, why don't you toss this right back to Com. Air Int., where it belongs? I've held the fort, and so far I haven't goofed. Well, to make a long story short, I lost. So until the civilians make up their minds what to do with you, I remain in charge. And why? Because I am the innocent victim of conspiracy and intrigue. Ever since Korea, Claypoole has been trying to get my corner office with the three windows and the big waiting room, and I tell you, he'll stop at nothing . . . but I don't want to bore you with my problems.

(*Takes a cigar from the coffee table.* KRETON *lights it for him*)

KRETON

But I love having you bore me. You do it so beautifully.

POWERS

Well, thank you, sir.

KRETON

And may I say you have already earned an undying place in the roster of your country's military statesmen.

POWERS

*(Beaming)*

Only my duty.

KRETON

Nonsense; men have become President for less.

POWERS

You can say that again.

KRETON

*(Thoughtfully)*

No, I think once is enough.

POWERS

Anyway, the big thing is you're here and, as of now at least, you're mine. And I know you will understand my position and cooperate to the fullest.

KRETON

Gladly.

(POWERS, *relieved, begins to assert himself*)

POWERS

Now, right off the bat, you can forget this taking-charge-of-the-world business. That's out. Not even the civilians would sit still for that. So just put it out of your mind. All right? All right. Now, ordinarily with a new weapon like yourself . . .

KRETON

Me? A new weapon?

POWERS

Oh, sure, sure. Forgot to tell you: You've been classified as a weapon. Later on we'll probably be able to figure out some peacetime uses for you, but right now I want to tell you that Central Intelligence was tickled pink when they heard you could read minds. And that force-field thing you do — well, that just about puts radar out of business. Now, ordinarily we'd ship you down to the proving ground at Aberdeen — run you through some tests — but out of respect for your status as an alleged mammal, we'll skip that phase. But we *will* expect you to provide us with a comprehensive list of your various unusual powers — we'll need sixteen copies for immediate distribution. You can get on that right away. All right? All right. We'll want to announce your arrival ourselves. Want to see you get the best possible break, publicity-wise. Roger will be very helpful in that area.

KRETON

(*At last breaking in*)

No, no, I'm sorry. I couldn't allow that. No one must know I'm here. It would spoil everything. I can't allow you to print one single word.

POWERS

(*Forgetting himself*)

Mr. Kreton, just how do you think you're going to stop us?

(KRETON *starts to make his magic gesture.* POWERS *ricochets toward the bar*)

POWERS

(*Alarm*)

All right. All right. Just as you say. You're probably right, too. (*Desperate rationalization*) We announce we have you, then the damned Russians claim they've got one too . . . only better. . . . They haven't got one, have they?

KRETON

No, I'm the only one down here, I'm happy to say.

POWERS

Well, good. Good. And don't you ever forget, Mr. Kreton, that you are a discovery of the United States. And I don't mind saying, right to your face, that in my opinion you — just you alone — are worth all the H bombs in the world combined.

KRETON

Ah, but I make so much less noise!

POWERS

(*New thought*)

Well, that's true.

KRETON

What a nice general you are! I'm so glad I got you instead of Lieutenant General Son-of-a-bitch Claypoole!

POWERS

(*Pleased*)

Yes, well, now, let's get started on that old list, eh?

(ROGER *runs in from the porch, wearing his hat, carrying a briefcase*)

ROGER

Powers!

POWERS

Hey, now! Wait a minute, Roger; this is a top-level security meeting. No unauthorized personnel . . . either military or civilian.

ROGER

(*Desperately*)

Powers! Will you listen to me? The Russians have discovered *antigravity!*

POWERS

Antigravity?

ROGER

At eleven twenty-six this morning every rifle in the free world was raised fifteen feet in the air for thirty seconds and then lowered again. It's the Russians, obviously.

POWERS

(*Aghast*)

Who else?

KRETON

(*Curiously*)

Are you quite sure only *your* rifles were raised?

ROGER

Apparently. There's been a complete news blackout east of the Rhine. Tom, this is it: tactical exercise preparatory to invasion.

(POWERS *has begun to die with terror*)

KRETON

Oh, General, how wonderful this must be for you! Now you'll have your chance to fight them with hydrogen bombs, with poison gas, with broken beer bottles if necessary . . . to fight them in the alleys, to fight them on the beaches . . .

POWERS

(*Unamused by this reprise*)

Yes, yes, well, yes. . . . Rog, you say they raised *all* the rifles?

ROGER

Every last one of them, Tom.

POWERS

(*The mind slowly improvises*)

I suppose, Mr. Kreton, that if they could raise rifles, there's no *practical* reason why they couldn't successfully raise heavier ordnance, too? I mean machine guns, tanks, battleships — I don't suppose it would affect aircraft, of course; I mean, if they're up there already, which they would be . . .

(*The enormity of it all is too much for him. He sits heavily on the sofa*)

KRETON

Of course antigravity is all a matter of concentration, really. Quite simple once you get the hang of it.

ROGER

(*Sudden idea*)

Mr. Kreton! I'm doing my broadcast here at home tonight. And

I think it might be a very inspiring thing for Mother and Father America if you'd come on as my special guest and . . .

KRETON

Oh, no, I'm afraid I couldn't do *that!* But why don't you interview General Powers? He'd make a splendid guest.

(POWERS *brightens at the thought*)

POWERS

Well, sure, Rog, be happy to go on with you, help out in any way I can. Don't hesitate to call on me.

ROGER

(*Stricken*)

Well, possibly . . . possibly. . . . I'll have to call New York, see if I can get network clearance . . .

(*Goes out the hall door*)

POWERS

(*Puzzled*)

Clearance? Well, that's old Rog for you. . . . Now, Mr. Kreton, we've got a lot of work to do — don't want to waste any time — so let's get started, shall we? Now, the desk is in the library. Remember? And the library is right in there. (*Briefcase in hand, he leads* KRETON *into the study* ) Sit right down here. (KRETON *sits at desk* ) Now, if you would be so good as to start drawing up that list we agreed on . . . looks like we'll be using you sooner than we thought, eh? (POWERS *had given* KRETON *a pen which he holds in the air like a wand* ) You do know how to write, don't you?

KRETON

Oh, I love writing.

*(Makes elaborate circles and loops, to* POWERS's *bewilderment)*

POWERS

*(Uneasily)*

Good. Try to be as brief and concise as possible. Now, while you're scribbling away, I'll be up with Rog, planning the big broadcast for tonight. *(Opens briefcase)* Here're some more carbons.

*(Stacks the carbon paper on the desk)*

KRETON

Thank you.

POWERS

*(Suddenly)*

Say, you're not worried about this antigravity thing, are you?

KRETON

Oh, dear, no!

POWERS

Glad to hear it. We'll give 'em the old *(Imitates* KRETON's *gesture)*, eh?

*(*KRETON *giggles.* POWERS *laughs happily and goes.* KRETON *makes more circles with the pen. Then* ROSEMARY *calls to him from the window. He crosses to her, picks her up )*

KRETON

*There* you are, Rosemary! Were you listening all the time? Oh, you are wicked! But isn't it thrilling? One incident and the whole world is now aquiver! You found a mouse? Oh, how luscious. (*He walks into living room, cat in hand* ) Well, you have your hobby and I have mine. . . . Oh, I know you don't like people, but then, I don't like mice. *Chacun à son goût.* I simply dote on people. . . . Why? Because of their primitive addiction to violence, because they seethe with emotions which I find bracing and intoxicating. For countless ages I have studied them and now I'm here to experience them firsthand, to wallow shamelessly in their steaming emotions . . . and to have fun, fun, fun! . . . How? You *were* listening, weren't you? Well, I do believe I have started a war. At least, I hope so. After all, that's what I came down here to see! I mean, it's the one thing they do really well. Oh, I can't think what will happen next. (*He crosses to a globe of the world. He ponders it thoughtfully* ) Rosemary, advise me. Do I dare? Yes? Well, then why not go whole hog? Metaphor! (*He gestures, and the globe explodes. He looks at it in wild alarm* ) Oh, dear! That was a bit much. . . . But very pretty!

(*Laughing delightedly, he accomplishes a small jig*)

CURTAIN

## SCENE TWO

## ACT TWO

### SCENE TWO

*Early evening of the same day as the previous scene.*

*The aide is at the porch door. Reba watches the television set in the study. In the living room, Roger is on the air. He wears his toupee. One television technician holds a boom mike while the other operates a portable camera. Powers sits out of camera range, nervously studying a massive script.*

ROGER

Mother and Father America, have you had your milk today? Pour yourself a glass of Cloverdale, the milkier milk . . . look at that white foamy goodness, rich in those lactic acids your body needs. (*Puts milk down untouched*) And now, what sort of day has it been? Well, it's been quite a day. Not since those dark hours before Munich has the free world been so close to the precipice of total war. As you know, this morning at eleven twenty-six the Russians launched a new antigravity force which suspended all the rifles in the free world some fifty feet off the ground. Then, late this afternoon at the U.N., Moscow, in an obvious move to avert suspicion, accused the United States of lifting all the rifles in the Communist world one hundred seven feet off the ground. Meanwhile unrest has marked the day all around the globe. In Burma, angry crowds sawed the American minister in half and committed other diplomatic improprieties. . . . But one thing is certain — in the next few hours we will know the answer to the big question: war or peace. And I predict that no matter what — and get this, Nikita Kruschev and your gang — Mother and Father America are ready. Come what may, we are ready. And now for our special guest — a man who needs no introduction, a great American soldier: Major General Tom Powers. Come on over here, Tom boy. (POWERS *stumbles into view. Hearty handclasp. Both men wreathed in good will*) Howdy, partner. (*To audience*) We were at Harvard Business School together. I don't like to think how many years ago that was. (*Laughs*)

POWERS

(*Laughs*)

A long time ago, Roger.

ROGER

(*Laughs*)

Yes, a long time ago. It's been quite a career for Major General Tom Powers.

POWERS

(*Carefully*)

Yes, Rog, I am happy to say that the Laundry Corps has finally come of age.

ROGER

What's your job now, Tom boy?

POWERS

Well, Roger, actually, it's a bit hush-hush. At the moment I'm on detached service from the Laundry Corps . . .

ROGER

(*Quickly*)

You can trust me, Tom boy. I'm sure there aren't any spies listening in tonight. (*Both laugh long at this pleasantry* ) Well, that's very interesting, very illuminating. Now, Tom boy, what is *your* considered opinion of the present crisis?

POWERS

(*Smiles*)

Well, Roger, it doesn't look good.

ROGER

It doesn't look good, Tom?

POWERS

(*Chuckling*)

No, Roger, it doesn't look good.

ROGER

Do you believe we've done everything possible to avert war?

POWERS

Well . . .

ROGER

(*Winding up; to audience*)

I don't need to tell you that we're getting the inside story, the big over-all picture tonight from Major General Tom Powers.

Now tell me, Tom boy, what do you think about this antigravity weapon?

POWERS

I . . .

ROGER

(*Wound up*)

Despite the best efforts of American science, wouldn't you say they've stolen a march on us?

POWERS

Well, I . . .

ROGER

(*Inexorable*)

Indeed they have! But it's only temporary. And, as always, American know-how will catch up. Now for the big question: if the enemy were to strike suddenly — tonight, say — would we be ready for them?

POWERS

(*Ready for his big moment*)

I . . .

ROGER

(*Ineluctable*)

We have never been more ready and I predict that antigravity will never be a match for the morale of a free people. (*Technician makes television speed-up gesture* ) Which winds up another half hour of "Roger Spelding Faces the News." Mother and Father America, have you had your milk today? (*He pours slop-*

*pily, hastily* ) Remember, this Cloverdale seal is your guarantee the milk you serve your family is *milkier*. Thank you and good night.

TECHNICIAN

On the button, Mr. Spelding.

ROGER

Thank you, boys.

TECHNICIAN

Good night, Mr. Spelding.

POWERS

(*Crushed*)

Real treat to be on, Rog.

ROGER

Well, it may be a treat for you, but it's a living hell for me! The first visitor from outer space right here in this house . . . and what do I do? I interview *you!*

(KRETON'S *voice mysteriously fills the room*)

KRETON'S VOICE

General Powers!

POWERS

Yes, sir!

KRETON'S VOICE

Do bring me the figures on radioactive fallout.

POWERS

Yes, sir!

*(There is a sound of running water)*

KRETON'S VOICE

And a sponge.

POWERS

A sponge, sir?

KRETON'S VOICE

Yes. I'm having my first bath . . . an extraordinary sensation!

POWERS

Right away. (*To* AIDE) Hup!

(POWERS *and* AIDE *dash into the study, as* ELLEN *and* CONRAD *enter from the porch*)

ROGER

(*Disapproving*)

So there you are, Ellen.

ELLEN

Hello, Daddy.

ROGER

I assume that once again you and Conrad were too busy to watch my broadcast.

KRETON'S VOICE

Do hurry, General.

POWERS

(*In the study*)

I'm coming, I'm coming.

(POWERS, *papers in hand, followed by the* AIDE, *pushes into the hall;* ROGER *calls to him*)

ROGER

There's a sponge right in the bathroom.

POWERS

(*To* AIDE *as they dash upstairs*)

There's a sponge right in the bathroom!

CONRAD

What?

ROGER

Extraordinary! Really extraordinary! While civilization crashes around our heads, Mr. Kreton takes a bath and you two are off Heaven knows where.

CONRAD

Ellen was helping me prune my walnut trees.

ELLEN

Then we had a picnic. It was lovely.

CONRAD

Except for this dumb soldier, who had to go with us.

ROGER

Well, while you were lunching alfresco, the entire international situation was exploding. We are on the brink of another world war . . . and I suggest, Conrad, that you get back into uniform right away. The Army will need every man it can get. I'm sure Powers will let you out of here to join up. After all, you young chaps need your sleep as much as us old gaffers do. So enlist. Right away. Before tonight, if possible.

(*A torrent of water sounds from above*)

KRETON'S VOICE

Oh, Mr. Spelding.

ROGER

Yes, sir.

KRETON'S VOICE

I seem to have turned on the shower by mistake, such a complex mechanism. General Powers wants to know if you'll bring us a mop.

ROGER

A mop? Yes, sir. Right away, sir!

(*Dashes off through hall door*)

ELLEN

The brink of another world war? What is my father talking about?

CONRAD

Honey, according to your father, this makes the sixth world war we've had since Dewey was elected President.

(ELLEN *sits on the sofa*)

ELLEN

I'm sure there won't be another war. There just couldn't be, could there?

(CONRAD *goes to her*)

CONRAD

Well, with all these maniacs running around loose, you can't ever tell; so let's get married. We'll go in town, find a justice of the peace and . . .

ELLEN

Darling, I can't marry you.

CONRAD

Why not?

ELLEN

Well, for one thing, Daddy would be furious.

CONRAD

Daddy? Let me tell you about Daddy: You don't know him the way I do. This may come as a shock, but last night your father tried to kill me. About midnight, I woke up all of a sudden and there he was, standing over me with this crazy gleam in his eyes, holding this pillow all ready to smother me to death. So I sat up and said, real calm, "Hi, Mr. Spelding, and what can I do for you, sir?" Then he just lost his head and started screaming. "Mayberry," he screamed, "if you don't stop making those funny noises in your sleep" — me who never makes a sound — "I'll ram this pillow down your throat." And he would, too. I could tell by those crazy eyes of his rolling around. So don't you see, honey,

I can't go back to that room again, and that's why we got to get married.

ELLEN

But Daddy . . .

CONRAD

Look, if Daddy thought it would get me out of his bedroom tonight, he'd sell you into white slavery.

ELLEN

Oh, darling, I just can't marry you. Not really.

CONRAD

Why not . . . really?

ELLEN

Well, for one thing you don't have any . . . drive.

CONRAD

No drive? With my own two hands, I built my house . . .

ELLEN

I didn't mean it that way. What I mean by drive is, well, someone who has . . . lots of energy and someone who's, well, famous . . .

CONRAD

You mean someone like Mother and Father America's least accurate news analyst?

ELLEN

Oh, I know there's a lot wrong with Daddy . . . but the point is, Conrad, you don't even *want* to be rich and famous. You're not even worldly.

CONRAD

Not worldly! I spent a year at the University of Virginia. I majored in "worldly."

ELLEN

Darling, you're sweet. But maybe what I really want . . . what I really need . . . is somebody who'd drag me around by the hair . . .

CONRAD

All you have to do is let it grow.

*(Seizes her by the hair. Tangled in one another's arms, they fall back onto the sofa)*

ELLEN

Oh, Conrad . . .

*(She relaxes weakly into his arms as* KRETON, *dressed as a Confederate general, enters from the hallway)*

KRETON

Oh, you've started . . . good! Don't mind me. I won't make a sound. I'll just sit here, and watch.

*(*KRETON *sits attentively as the children untangle. The* AIDE *crosses unobtrusively from hall to the porch, where he resumes guard duty)*

ELLEN

*(Severely)*

We've been through that this morning, Mr. Kreton. It isn't nice . . . and what're you wearing?

KRETON

Dashing, isn't it? I'm a Confederate general. I was planning to wear it at Bull Run. . . . Why aren't *you* in uniform, Conrad?

CONRAD

Because I'm not going to fight anybody. And just what's going on, anyway?

ELLEN

Yes. This morning I thought you said you were going to take over the world. Well, why haven't you? You've had all day . . .

KRETON

I decided not to. More fun to observe.

CONRAD

I don't get it. This morning everything was nice and peaceful and now all of a sudden everybody wants me to run out and join the Army.

KRETON

*(Carefully)*

Well, you see, it's those wicked Russians. They have this dreadful new weapon. And you know how mechanically minded they are.

CONRAD

And that's why we've got to fight them?

KRETON

Apparently. (*Nervously*) Well, don't look so accusingly at me. It's not my fault.

ELLEN

But you could stop it.

KRETON

No, no, no. That wouldn't be right. Stand on your own two feet. Rally to the colors. Conrad, to arms!

ELLEN

Mr. Kreton, Conrad doesn't believe in fighting.

KRETON

(*To* CONRAD)

But . . . how will you answer your children when they ask, "Daddy, what did *you* do in the big war?"

CONRAD

Oh, no, not that one.

KRETON

Has that argument been propounded before?

CONRAD

Yes.

KRETON

It *seemed* emotionally correct. The pitch was perfect. Conrad, I don't entirely understand you. Do you love your country?

CONRAD

Uh-huh.

KRETON

Then don't you want to slaughter its enemies?

CONRAD

(*Shaking his head*)

Uh-huh.

KRETON

That is the wrong answer. That is not a proper mid-twentieth-century sentiment. Come now, Conrad, you know that deep down inside you're a warm, passionate human being like the rest. After all, the Jefferson Davis Motel, Cottage D . . . the four telephone books . . .

CONRAD

That has nothing to do with it.

KRETON

Oh, yes, it does. Sex and aggression — exactly the same thing. I'm sure in your heart you want to fight side by side with your buddies.

ELLEN

No, Conrad's different.

KRETON

But surely he has the same patriotic responses as General Powers and your father and (*Points to* AIDE *at the door*) that young man there.

CONRAD

No, I just want to be let alone. I'm a peace-loving man who grows English walnuts.

KRETON

Until emotional stimuli are applied. Such as (*Recites*) the Declaration of Independence; "with malice toward none . . ."; Mount Rushmore; Ars Gratia Artis. . . . Conrad, aren't your hackles rising?

CONRAD

No, my hackles are unstirred.

KRETON

(*Sharply*)

Oh, don't be so exasperating. You're supposed to respond violently to certain combinations of words and music. All primitives can be lashed to fever pitch by selected major chords.

CONRAD

Not me.

ELLEN

He's right. And you really ought to be proud of him. I am, generally.

KRETON

Proud of someone who perversely tries *not* to be what he is? But of course he's the same as everyone else. He has to be. Look at that tiny cortex! This rebellion is simply an act of the will, nothing more.

CONRAD

Maybe it is, but I believe in self-control. Nobody's rousing me to fight anybody.

KRETON

May I have a go at it?

ELLEN

(*Warningly*)

Now . . . no tricks.

(KRETON *arranges* CONRAD *center stage.* CONRAD, *puzzled, stands, arms at his sides*)

KRETON

No tricks. I shall stir him emotionally . . . in his own terms. (*Clears his throat*) Relax, Conrad. Better get your hanky out. You will probably cry, but it's for your own sake. (*Begins to sing emotionally*)

There's a long, long trail a-winding
Into the land of my dreams,
Where the nightingales are singing
And a white moon beams.

(*No reaction from* CONRAD. KRETON *then crosses to telephone. He sings into it*)

Hello, Central, give me No Man's Land.
My daddy's there . . . my mama told me.

(*Blends into*)

Over there, over there,
Send the word, send the word over there,
For the Yanks are coming, the Yanks are coming,
With drums rum tumming everywhere! *

(*He has marched back to the impassive* CONRAD. *He takes his pulse: no response. He pulls out more stops* ) Abraham Lincoln. Ann Rutledge. "The world may little note nor long remember . . ." Barbara Frietchie.

(CONRAD *looks at* ELLEN *with alarm.* KRETON *takes this as a chink in his armor. He bellows*)

When Johnny comes marching home again, tra-la, tra-la,
When Johnny comes marching home again, tra-la, tra-la.

(*Intones*)

In Texas, Davy Crockett stood by his guns. Remember the Alamo! Remember the Maine! Remember Errol Flynn on the Burma Road! (*Takes* CONRAD's *pulse again: it has begun to leap. Quickly* KRETON *maneuvers him into a chair. Then he kneels beside him. This is the heavy artillery. Sings*)

One of our planes was missing, two hours overdue.
One of our planes was missing, with all its gallant crew.
The radio sets were humming, they waited for a word;
Then a voice broke through the humming and this is what they heard:
Comin' in on a wing and a prayer . . .
Comin' in on a wing and a prayer . . .
Tho' there's one motor gone, we can still carry on,
Comin' in on a wing and a prayer! †

(*The tears are now streaming down* KRETON'S *face as he breaks off. A heart-rending moment. Then he turns to* CONRAD, *hardly able to contain his emotion* ) And, Conrad, it's for Mother.

CONRAD

(*Reasonably*)

Then let Mother go fight.

ELLEN

She'd love it, too. Conrad's mother was a major in the WACs. She's terribly military.

CONRAD

A first-class fighting woman.

(KRETON *is shattered*)

KRETON

Is nothing sacred? I don't want to seem a sentimental old silly, but, well, I would've enlisted like a shot if someone had appealed to me the way I did to you. I can't think *what* went wrong. Your pulse was leaping like a hero.

ELLEN

You really ought to leave him alone, Mr. Kreton.

KRETON

Of course I admit I'm not in very good voice.

ELLEN

That's not true. You sang very nicely; some of it was awfully touching.

KRETON

No, no, you're just saying that. It was an awful bust.

(*In the doorway, the* AIDE, *reduced to quiet tears, blows his nose*)

AIDE

*I* thought it was wonderful, sir!

KRETON

(*Startled*)

Oh! Well, aren't you nice to say so! (*To* CONRAD) Now there . . . *there* is a man. Just listen to *him.*

(*Gestures*)

AIDE'S MIND

(*Imitates the staccato sound of a machine gun*)

This one's for me. (*Machine gun again*) And this one's for that babe with the crazy build. Yeah, I been watching you shaking it around this house. And you been watching me, watching you, driving me mad.

ELLEN

Why, he's thinking about *me!*

AIDE

(*Coming to*)

I didn't say a word, miss.

(*But his mind is out of control*)

AIDE'S MIND

We don't need words, woman, not you and me. We both of us knew that night old Lead-Ass and me walked into this house and you gave me the eye. Bells rang. The earth moved. It was like there was nobody in the world, just you and me, and the black, burning night exploding like a thousand Roman candles . . .

KRETON

(*Entranced*)

A thousand what?

AIDE

Roman candles. You know.

(*He ineffectually pantomimes a Roman candle*)

CONRAD

(*Dangerously*)

I propose, sir, you discontinue this line of thought.

ELLEN

Oh, no, no! It's fascinating . . . really.

AIDE

I'm sorry, miss.

ELLEN

That's all right. I know you can't help it.

KRETON

My dear, you must marry him *too*. I'm sure the three of you would make a lovely couple.

CONRAD

Come on, let's knock all this off . . . right now.

ELLEN

Conrad! (*Rises*) Don't be so stuffy. Actually, you should be flattered men find me attractive!

(*She faces the alarmed* AIDE)

AIDE'S MIND

And your hungry eyes, begging me, imploring me, entreating me to take you in my powerful arms, my potent thighs . . .

CONRAD

(*Furious*)

Now, damn it!

AIDE'S MIND

Like a great sea surging, I take you, whimpering with ecstasy . . .

(CONRAD, *with a scream, swings at the* AIDE *and misses. They fall to the floor, fighting wildly.* KRETON *is delighted.* ELLEN *is furious but excited*)

ELLEN

Conrad, stop that! Stop that this minute!

KRETON

Ah, the vibrations! You could cut them with a knife!

(CONRAD *is now on his back, being pounded*)

ELLEN

Conrad, stop! . . . Well, hit him! Conrad, don't let him do that to you! Hit him back! (*To* KRETON) Will you stop this?

KRETON

Not for the world! I love it. They love it. You love it!

(*With a cry,* ELLEN *hurls herself onto the fighting men*)

KRETON

That's right, Ellen! Save him! Save him!

(*Now all three roll about the floor, while* KRETON *jumps up and down with excitement. In the midst of this confusion,* POWERS, *carrying a mop, and* ROGER, *carrying a bucket, enter from the hall*)

POWERS

(*Bellowing*)

What's going on here?

(KRETON *tries to shove* POWERS *into the fight*)

KRETON

Jump in. . . . Jump in, quickly! They're tiring!

(*But* POWERS *assumes a military stance*)

POWERS

Captain! Captain! Attention!

(*The* AIDE *leaps to his feet and stands at attention.* ELLEN *and* CONRAD *stagger to their feet*)

ROGER

(*Delighted by the debacle*)

Conrad's gone berserk! I knew he would. That boy is deranged.

POWERS

(*To* AIDE)

What are you doing to those two civilians?

AIDE

Protecting myself, sir.

ELLEN

It was his mind . . .

CONRAD

(*Gasping*)

A foul, filthy mind . . .

ROGER

(*To* ELLEN)

Conrad turned on you, didn't he, Ellen? I suppose he tried to kill you.

POWERS

(*Sternly addressing the* AIDE)

Captain, I will have discipline. You understand me? Discipline. What is an army, I ask you, but discipline? Theirs not to reason why; theirs but to do or die. . . . Straighten that blouse. Return to your post. (*The* AIDE *goes out onto porch as* POWERS *shouts after him*) And tomorrow you go back to Claypoole, where you belong.

(*Throws the mop after the* AIDE)

ROGER

Don't be too hard on the lad, Tom boy. He was defending my little girl here.

ELLEN

Oh, no, he wasn't. "Whimpering with ecstasy," indeed.

KRETON

I'm limp with excitement. It all started when I tried to appeal to this boy to join the Army in his country's hour of peril.

ROGER

(*To* CONRAD)

Slacker is an ugly word, Conrad.

ELLEN

Conrad's a pacifist and willing to fight for it.

KRETON

A pacifist with a hard right, a stealthy left jab and a sly knee to the groin. . . . And may I add, that in his heart there was blood lust.

POWERS

Well, I can't let the troops rape and loot. Doesn't look right for the Laundry Corps. Captain!

(*Goes out onto porch.* ELLEN *caresses the battered* CONRAD)

ELLEN

Darling, where does it hurt?

CONRAD

All over.

ELLEN

Poor angel.

(*She kisses him*)

ROGER

Ellen, go to your room.

ELLEN

Certainly not. I'm going to marry Conrad. Tonight.

(ROGER *is appalled*)

ROGER

You . . . you would voluntarily share the bed of this . . . Oh, Ellen, you can't. It's a living hell. I know.

ELLEN

I'll take my chances.

ROGER

Is this your last word on the subject?

ELLEN

Yes, Daddy. Wasn't Conrad simply wonderful!

KRETON

(*With pleasure*)

Bestial . . . absolutely bestial! Complete reversion to type. Couldn't be better!

ROGER

Then I wash my hands of both of you.

CONRAD

Now, don't do that, sir. After all, you may have lost a roommate, but you've gained a son . . . Dad.

(*Goes to embrace* ROGER, *who holds the bucket between them*)

ROGER

Revolting! Go! Go!

ELLEN

Come on, darling!

(ELLEN *and* CONRAD *go out the porch door.* POWERS *re-enters; he has mysteriously regained the mop. The* AIDE *is again at his post*)

ROGER

She'll never sleep again. My own child!

(*Goes upstairs*)

POWERS

(*To the* AIDE)

Detail a man as escort. This is a military establishment and must be run as such.

(*Tries to salute, but the mop is in the way. Distraught, he puts it down*)

AIDE

(*Saluting*)

Yes, sir, General.

(*Follows* ELLEN *and* CONRAD *off stage*)

KRETON

I do wish they'd have a proper wedding, with all the barbaric splendor of their tribe, but . . . Oh, General! I completely forgot to tell them the great news.

POWERS

What news is that, sir?

KRETON

War! I have arranged a sneak attack for tonight. The good ones always start with a sneak attack.

POWERS

*You* arranged this?

KRETON

Yes, in exactly forty-seven minutes. Zero hour. You see, I was so troubled by that antigravity, I couldn't sit still. And since no one else was doing anything except talk, I took the bull by the horns and launched the bombers myself.

(POWERS *is stunned. He pours himself a heavy drink*)

POWERS

You? Well, at last the old eagle strikes.

(*He sinks into a chair*)

KRETON

Exactly. Isn't it thrilling?

POWERS

(*Deflated*)

Yes, thrilling.

(KRETON *looks at him curiously*)

KRETON

I must say you don't seem awfully keen.

POWERS

Oh, no, I'm keen. . . . "Into the valley of death rode the six hundred," and all that.

KRETON

Your spirits are flagging. Oh, General, do buck up! (*Sighs*) Well, here we go again.

(*Kneels beside the general — exactly the same position he took with* CONRAD. *He hands* POWERS *a handkerchief. Then he sings*)

There's a long, long trail a-winding
Into the land of my dreams.

(POWERS *begins to cry*)

Where the nightingales are singing
And a white moon beams.

(*On the last line,* POWERS *has joined him: a high barbershop tenor*)

CURTAIN

# ACT THREE

## ACT THREE

*It is half an hour later.*

*The aide is arranging a large map of South America on the mantelpiece while General Powers, holding a drink, directs operations. In the study, a wireless radio has been installed. Maps are strewn about the floor of the living room.*

POWERS

A little more to the left. (*The* AIDE *moves the map to the right* ) I said left, Captain. You do know left from right, don't you?

AIDE

Yes, sir.

(*Moves the map into place*)

POWERS

You must've learned something at West Point besides treachery and conniving . . .

AIDE

(*Softly*)

Yes, sir.

POWERS

Looting and raping.

AIDE

Yes, sir.

(KRETON *dashes down the stairs, his arms full of toy airplanes*)

KRETON

What a nice war room this is getting to be! (*He hands* POWERS *two airplanes* ) Now, these are your bombers, General, and you're the enemy.

POWERS

I'm what?

KRETON

Just for now. This will give you an idea of what's going to happen in seventeen minutes. . . . So pay attention. This is my war plan. (*He puts planes on coffee table* ) Here is my fighter base and that's the enemy's bomber base under the chair. (*He indicates the chair by the door.* POWERS *looks at him, mystified* ) Well, go on, General. Bomber base. That's you. Under the chair. (POWERS *reluctantly arranges his planes under the chair* ) Now this is Buenos Aires behind the sofa and the sofa itself is the Andes. And the captain's standing on Washington. (*The* AIDE *leaps away* ) It's a bit complicated . . . but fun! Now, six hours before zero hour, I take off. (*He takes off with a zooming noise.* POWERS *watches in alarm* ) Then the enemy's radar picks me up over the Andes. You be radar, Captain.

POWERS

(*Curtly*)

Well, go on. Be radar.

(*The* AIDE *picks up portable antenna from the television set and puts it on his head. Happily, he makes beep-beep noises*)

KRETON

Then the enemy takes off. Well, go on, General. You're the enemy. Take off. (POWERS, *arms spread, takes off, buzzing hoarsely.* KRETON *circles him ominously.* POWERS *retreats around the sofa.* KRETON *leaps onto the sofa* ) Now I'm coming at you out of the sun. We're over Utah now. I'm gaining altitude.

(*Leaps from the sofa.* POWERS *darts to the door*)

AIDE

Look out, General! Enemy fighters at two o'clock!

(KRETON *is upon* POWERS )

KRETON

Now we have a dog fight! (POWERS *fights valiantly with his planes. But he is clearly doomed* ) And now I blow you up. BOOM! (POWERS *imitates the sound of a plane hurtling to earth* ) Clobbered! A glorious victory!

(KRETON *flies his planes serenely back to the coffee table. He lands them and sits down, delighted*)

POWERS

Take off that radar, Captain. Police the area. I'm going to have discipline around here or know the reason why.

(*The* AIDE *removes antenna. He starts to pick up the scattered maps and airplanes*)

KRETON

Oh, and I shall need some ground troops. I shall want three boxes of soldiers. Do get them. Right away. (*The* AIDE *looks bewildered*) You know: *little* ones. Coldstream Guards will do. We'll put them over there by the television. That's London.

POWERS

On the double, Captain. Priority 1-A.

(*The* AIDE *runs out porch door*)

KRETON

Well, what do you think of my plan, General?

POWERS

Am I to understand that this, ah, tactical demonstration is for real?

KRETON

Of course, "for real." I confess there were times today when I wanted to tell you, but then I thought: No! let it come as a wonderful surprise for General.

POWERS

Well, it's certainly a surprise.

KRETON

And now let's go listen to the wireless in the bathroom.

(*Leads* POWERS *into the study*)

POWERS

That's the study.

KRETON

So it is. I keep making these curious blunders. It must be all the excitement. The world's beginning to vibrate . . . ever so thrilling!

(*Continues to play with his airplanes while* POWERS *listens to the headphones*)

POWERS

I guess you're right. Complete mobilization in Russia.

KRETON

How exciting!

(*Wireless signals.* POWERS *listens again*)

POWERS

Operation Meat Chopper, Phase One, to be activated in Argentina at twenty hundred. Like you said . . . this is it. (*He pours himself a drink* ) Sure I couldn't interest you in a little snort?

KRETON

Oh, no. No, thank you. (*Curiously*) You must be terribly thirsty. That's your fourth "snort" since the broadcast.

POWERS

(*Laughs amiably*)

Hey, now! No counting! Actually, relaxes tension.

KRETON

Are you tense?

POWERS

Of course. War. All keyed up. Alert. Eve of battle.

KRETON

Do have another. I enjoy watching you drink fermented vegetation. It's having such an effect on your vibrations. (*Pours him another drink*) Here you are. Imbibe your fire water.

POWERS

Well, thanks. Here's mud in your eye.

(*Drinks*)

KRETON

What a happy thought!

POWERS

(*Suddenly confidential*)

You know, for a while there last night you had me worried. Yes, sir, you won't believe it, but I damn near had you figured out as one of those . . . well, fellow travelers — a parlor pink — and I don't mind telling you I was pretty depressed. Upset. Scared. But now . . . well, you're okay (*He makes "okay" gesture with thumb and forefinger* ) in my book. We're in this together . . . comrades-in-arms.

KRETON

Buddies?

POWERS

Buddies. (*They clasp hands warmly. Then* POWERS *turns grave* ) I suppose we're going to win *right away*, aren't we?

KRETON

(*Evasively*)

I should think so.

POWERS

They've got the bomb, too, you know.

KRETON

Oh, I hope so!

(*He makes a ghastly bombing noise with one of the planes.* POWERS *slumps back in his chair*)

POWERS

(*Distraught*)

Don't. Please. I beg of you. (*More calmly*) My nerves . . . aren't very steady. I . . . well, I can't stand loud noises. Never could.

KRETON

But you're a soldier. I mean, all those wars you've been in. Why, the twentieth century is noted for its wars. . . . I can just see you now, bayonet in hand, leading your men through the barbed wire. . . . You have fought, haven't you?

POWERS

(*Slowly*)

Well, in the field, no. . . . You see, during the last war I got interested in laundry . . .

KRETON

Laundry?

POWERS

(*Warming up*)

Major logistical problem, laundry. Mobile units. Lot of big decisions to make in that area: kind of soap to use, things like that.

Decided finally on Snow Chip Flakes. Fine lather. Good detergent. Doesn't harm the fabric *and* has bluing already built in, which cut down our expenditures by two million dollars. All my idea. . . . Then of course you've heard of the Powers Mobile Laundry Unit K.

KRETON

No. You see, I don't like laundry.

POWERS

(*Growing progressively drunker, gets to his feet and becomes a mobile laundry unit*)

Well, you'll like this. All my own design, too. Put the laundry here. Dirtier the better. Stuff it in this opening. Slam the door shut. Pull the lever. Whoosh. Feel that hot water circulating? Now — and get this, it's automatic — soap is *shot* through the water. Detonated. Like puffed wheat. Got the idea from a cereal box, believe it or not. Snap, crackle, pop.

(*Wireless signals.* KRETON *answers it. He listens a moment, eagerly*)

KRETON

Some Chinese students have just blown up the Burmese Embassy in Peiping!

POWERS

Always admired the Chinese, great little people, born laundrymen. Naturals.

(KRETON *pours* POWERS *another drink*)

KRETON

Put some more mud in my eye.

POWERS

Well, all right. Just one more little drinkee. Good for the heart. (*Drinks up*)

KRETON

Something awfully peculiar is happening to your vibrations. . . . I do believe you're coming apart.

POWERS

Nonsense. Just relaxed. (*He tries to get up, but can't; he sits back heavily* ) Perfect coordination . . . of the nation. (*Secretly sings a stanza of the Marine Corps hymn*)

We're the finest ever seen.
And we glory in the title of United States Marines.

(*A long pause. Then, craftily*) I don't suppose *you* could do anything about that son of a bitch Claypoole, could you?

KRETON

Run over him with a car? Make it look like an accident?

POWERS

(*Sudden enthusiasm*)

Hey, now . . . ! (*Reality intervenes*) No, no, wouldn't look right. . . . But that's the right idea. (*Wireless signals.* POWERS *answers it unsteadily. He listens a moment: mounting horror* ) Great Scott!

KRETON

What's happened? Has the fighting begun?

POWERS

Worse than that. Strat. Air and Com. Air Int. have been combined. Emergency measure. And you know what that means? A whole new T.O. at the Pentagon. And do you know who will get my nice office with the three windows and the big mahogany desk and the waiting room? Claypoole! He's always wanted it. I tell you, Kreton, war is hell. That's what you fellows on the outside never realize.

KRETON

(*Soothingly*)

Now, now, it's not as bad as all that, I'm sure.

POWERS

No, I've seen it happen before too many times. Mr. Kreton, if there is one thing that destroys an army's morale and discipline, it is a major war. Everything goes to hell. Lose more damned sheets and pillow cases. Your laundry's a wreck! (*Tries to pour himself a drink: the bottle's empty. Still talking, he wanders into the living room.* KRETON *addresses himself to his war plan* ) And another thing, if it weren't for this war that you started, I'd've made permanent B.G. in January. But . . . well, from here on in it's strictly the blood-and-guts boys, while the really good men are lost in the shuffle. Combat generals, that's all you'll read about, tearing around in tanks and planes, spending money like water. They never met a payroll. (*He has found a bottle on the console and he returns to the study* ) I was on my way. Two stars. Three stars. Four stars. General of the Army Thomas R. Powers. Why not? And why not *President* Thomas R. Powers? (*He looks hopefully at* KRETON, *but* KRETON *merely smiles. Broken,* POWERS *turns away* ) But not now. No. (POWERS *is now in the hallway. He stands, crumbling, in the archway* ) I'll be sent overseas. Probably be killed: stray bullet, shrapnel, or one of those damned jeep drivers will run into something. And I used to be so happy. The Army was my home. (*Lachrymose*) My life. I loved that laundry. Mr. Kreton, I never wanted to be killed in a jeep. I . . . I just wanted to be President.

(*He turns and staggers upstairs, sobbing quietly.* KRETON *gathers his maps and goes into the living room*)

KRETON

Now, General Powers . . . (*He looks about, puzzled*) General? General Powers? (*Then he looks upstairs and understands*) I'm afraid poor General Powers is now adrift in the Land of Nod.

(CONRAD *enters. He is carrying* ELLEN *in his arms*)

KRETON

(*Alarmed*)

What's happened? An accident? Oh, but of course: ancient tribal custom: the warrior and his mate! (CONRAD *puts* ELLEN *down*) Oh, how I wish I could've been there, throwing rice! Anyway, you're back just in time for the sneak attack.

ELLEN

What sneak attack?

KRETON

*Tonight!* You remember that parlor trick this morning? Raising the rifles? Well, they think *you* did it and you think *they* did it — a typical chain of events. And now in roughly ten minutes — boom!

ELLEN

But you're going to stop it, aren't you?

KRETON

Stop it? My dear girl, I started it!

ELLEN

But you can't *want* a war . . .

KRETON

Of course I want a war. After all, I missed the Civil War, so the next best thing is to have one of my very own right here. (CONRAD *starts to remonstrate* ) Oh, Conrad, such thoughts! Why are you so perverse? Why can't you be like other boys? And I had such hopes for you this evening, rolling about the floor, strangling the captain. So did Ellen. After all, that's why she married you.

ELLEN

That wasn't the only reason . . .

CONRAD

(*Patiently*)

I admit sometimes we get overexcited, but nobody wants a war, because nobody wants to be killed.

KRETON

Well, every game has it penalties. I must say I would never have dreamed that one day I should be trying to convince a lower primate that he should behave like a lower primate. Dear Conrad, war is your specialty. Historians love you for it. I love you for it. After all, not only is it fun, it's creative! Your best scientific discoveries are made in wartime: the atom bomb, radar, luncheon meat. And think of all that travel! Getting away from home, making new acquaintances, indulging in amatory dalliance with strangers. So broadening. And then: the delirium of battle, the rush of adrenalin to the head as the trumpets sound ATTACK! Conrad, war is the principal art form of your race. You must force yourself to conform. Be uninhibited. Be yourself. Cruel. Relentless. Slash, bite, scratch . . . !

CONRAD

Look, I put it to you simply: I do not want to be killed. Ellen does not want to be killed. That tin-headed general does not want to be killed. Even Ellen's deranged father . . .

ELLEN

(*Angrily*)

Conrad!

KRETON

(*Delighted*)

You see? That's the way it starts. A quarrel. The air vibrates. My dear children, don't you know what you are? What you all are? Savages, bloodthirsty savages. That's why you're my hobby. That's why I've returned to the Dark Ages of an insignificant planet in a minor system circling a small and rather chilly sun to enjoy myself, to see you at your most typical . . .

CONRAD

So maybe we're *not* vegetables like you.

KRETON

(*Stung*)

I am not a vegetable. I am a mammal. The optimum work of nature.

(REBA *enters from kitchen*)

REBA

Oh, there you are, Mr. Kreton. Did Roger talk to you about anything?

KRETON

No, he hasn't asked me to leave yet. He forgot. But he'll remember tomorrow.

REBA

Oh, good. I must say one thing, if there's really going to be a war, which I doubt—you know how wrong Roger can be—we've got to be ready. (*To* KRETON) So I've been out buying little things for the house. And food for the deep freezer. (*To* CONRAD) Conrad, everything's in the car. Come on now and help me bring them in. (*Takes* CONRAD'S *arm*) It won't take a minute.

CONRAD

Mrs. Spelding, Ellen and I were married tonight.

REBA

Oh, Conrad, don't be silly. Now, come on. The rib roasts are in the back seat on the floor. The soldier is unloading the trunk and . . .

(*She leads* CONRAD *off*)

(ELLEN *stares at* KRETON *with horror and loathing*)

KRETON

Well, I must say this is your *best* vibration so far. Your very best. You are absolutely bathed in malevolence.

ELLEN

I could murder you.

KRETON

(*Excited*)

Go on! Go on! Denounce me.

ELLEN

Oh, you . . . you vampire!

KRETON

Eh? Vampire? Oh, I wouldn't dream of drinking blood. Not even yours, dear girl. Ugh!

ELLEN

Not blood. Emotions. You're going to blow us all up for the sake of your damned vibrations.

(*She collapses on the sofa and bursts into tears. He comforts her* )

KRETON

Now, now, poor little savage on a forgotten world, don't weep. Neither of us can help what you are. (*Then briskly*) So let's make the best of it, shall we? (*He sits beside her on the sofa* ) No tears. After all, you're married. Things are going great guns for everybody. Oh, I tell you it is a dream come true, my being here. If only Delton 4 could see me now!

ELLEN

Please, you can't do this . . . you just can't.

KRETON

(*Blithely ignoring her*)

He'll have a fit. You see, you're not supposed to have a war just yet. So now all the history books will have to be rewritten. Such a lark! And Delton 4 will be livid! He's the most awful fuss-budget about these things.

(ELLEN *controls her tears: an idea has occurred to her*)

ELLEN

But aren't they — Delton 4 and so on — aren't they looking for you?

KRETON

Of course they are, but the odds against being found *in time* are absolutely minuscule. Besides, knowing my passion for the Civil War, they'll look for me back in 1861, never dreaming I'm holed up in 1957. Practically one of the family.

ELLEN

If you wanted to get in touch with them, how would you?

KRETON

But I don't want to get in touch with them. Ever again.

ELLEN

But if you did.

KRETON

Through the mind, like everything else. Concentration. (*Gets to his feet, looks at the clock*) Well, I must get into my battle togs. Zero hour is almost upon us. I'm getting all shivery. (*He starts to go; then he stops. He smiles at her indulgently* ) I know that you think you can trick me into stopping this attack, but you can't, so don't even try. After all, I'm doing it for you. Also, if you're a *very* good girl, General Powers might just let you watch the bombing on the monitor: it should be dazzling! A whole forest of mushroom clouds! Delton 4 will expire with rage!

(KRETON, *singing gaily, runs upstairs.* ELLEN, *now intensely resolved, rises and crosses to the fireplace. She motions to the vase, concentrating. A sound of magic. The vase rises erratically; it hovers in the air, then drops back into place. Concentrating with all her might, she gets it to rise again. This time, after a number of odd gyrations, it settles. Desperate but hopeful,* ELLEN *returns to the sofa, her eyes shut as she murmurs over and over again*)

ELLEN

Delton 4 . . . Delton 4 . . . Delton 4 . . .

(*The* AIDE *runs in from the terrace, carrying three boxes of toy soldiers*)

AIDE

Beg your pardon, miss, have you seen the general?

ELLEN

(*Ignores him*)

Delton 4.

(*The* AIDE *decides that this may be the moment*)

AIDE

*(Shyly)*

I . . . I'm sorry about what happened. But I couldn't help what I was thinking. We're hot-blooded people where I come from. That's Marietta, Ohio. And I was born in April, too. That's Taurus, the bull. And sometimes, I guess, we just get carried away. Well, I'm sorry, miss . . . miss?

*(He decides at last that he is being snubbed. Sadly, he starts upstairs just as* POWERS *and* ROGER *descend, quarreling. The* AIDE *stands to one side, trying to get* POWERS' *attention)*

ROGER

You've *got* to let me break this story!

(POWERS *is rumpled, unmade . . . already hung-over)*

POWERS

Sorry, Rog, can't do it. The whole thing is out of hand. We've just got to keep cool heads, all of us.

ROGER

*(Growing desperation)*

Tom, you've got to help me!

(POWERS *makes ineffectual tidying gestures)*

POWERS

Rog, if you can keep your head when all about you are losing theirs and blaming it on you, then . . . I can't remember the rest, but anyway, old expendable Tom Powers resumes command.

AIDE

(*At last*)

General, I got the soldiers Mr. Kreton wanted. They didn't have any Coldstream Guards. But I got some Bengal Lancers and the Coronation of Queen Elizabeth with the gold coach and everything.

POWERS

All right, set them over there. (*Indicates television set*) That's London.

(AIDE *puts the boxes on the television set. All during this* ELLEN *continues to concentrate.* REBA *and* CONRAD *enter from the porch.* CONRAD *is loaded down with groceries. He goes on through to the hall.* REBA *turns on* ROGER *furiously* )

REBA

Roger, Ellen's married. And I suppose you knew it all along. . . . Well, I had a premonition something awful was going to happen today and now it has.

ROGER

Now, Reba.

REBA

It's too late for words, Roger. We have failed. You and I have failed as parents. And I hope you're satisfied. Now Ellen will never finish college.

(KRETON, *in campaign cap, cape and sword belt, charges into the room, brandishing his saber*)

KRETON

Tippecanoe and Tyler too! Charge!

REBA
(*Alarmed*)

Who?

KRETON

Early American war cry. (*To* POWERS) Everything on schedule?

POWERS

Tickety boo . . . tickety boo.

(*He chuckles weakly at this Anglicism*)

KRETON
(*Puzzled*)

Oh?

REBA

Now, Mr. Kreton, I don't want to be inhospitable, but . . .

KRETON
(*To* REBA)

I'll move tomorrow, I promise. But now I'm off to observe the bombing. I'll be back before morning. (*He turns to* ELLEN, *who is still concentrating, her eyes shut* ) And so, dear girl . . . (*He stops, suddenly appalled at what she is doing* ) Ellen, stop that! You stop that this minute! How dare you!

(CONRAD, *who has just returned from the hall, is the first to be aware of an increasing white radiance from the garden*)

CONRAD

Hey, look out there! (*He dashes to the door* ) It's another one!

ROGER

Another flying saucer!

*(The* AIDE *and* ROGER *join* CONRAD *on the porch.* ELLEN *does not stir.* REBA *waits resignedly in the living room.* KRETON, *after a frightened glance out the door, goes into the study and hides under the desk. As the light and noise from the new spaceship increase, the* AIDE, ROGER *and* CONRAD *retreat back into the living room as the handsome, suave* DELTON 4 *enters. He wears a morning suit and a bowler. The light fades. The sound stops. He pauses in the middle of the room)*

ROGER

*(Nervously)*

Any friend of Mr. Kreton is naturally a friend of ours . . .

*(But* DELTON 4 *ignores him; he crosses to* ELLEN*)*

DELTON 4

*(Softly)*

Thank you, Miss Spelding.

*(He crosses to the study and enters.* KRETON *sheepishly comes out of hiding. They communicate by odd sounds.* DELTON 4 *motions sternly for him to remove his sword. He does so reluctantly. In the living room, the terrestrials react excitedly — all but* ELLEN, *who is quietly playing Joan of Arc)*

REBA

*(The burden has become too great)*

I'm sorry. But this one goes to a hotel. *(She goes off down the hall)*

(*The* AIDE, *who has been staring out the door at the flying saucer, turns to* POWERS)

AIDE

Looks like a new model, General. Shouldn't we inspect it, sir?

POWERS

Why, yes. Yes, I think that's standard procedure. After all, he's an ally. Follow me, men.

(ROGER *and the* AIDE *run onto the porch and off stage.* POWERS *follows, uncertainly*)

CONRAD

What did he say to you?

ELLEN

He said, "Thank you, Miss Spelding."

CONRAD

For what?

ELLEN

(*Suddenly relieved*)

I sent for him and . . . oh, it's going to be all right now! Everything's going to be all right! (*She rises* ) Wait here, darling.

(*Goes into the study.* CONRAD *follows her.* DELTON 4, *without turning to acknowledge their presence, speaks*)

DELTON 4

You did the right thing, Miss Spelding. I am most grateful to you.

ELLEN

I just hope you can stop this war. There's supposed to be an attack . . .

DELTON 4

The war has already been stopped.

KRETON

Neither of you has any sense of fun.

DELTON 4

(*To* ELLEN)

You see, Kreton is a rarity among us. He is morally retarded and, like a child, he regards this world as his plaything. . . . Come, Kreton.

(DELTON 4, *carrying the saber, leads the way out of the study and into the living room*)

KRETON

(*Sulking*)

Like a child! Now, really! Simply because I have given pleasure and employment to a number of savages . . . very sweet savages.

DELTON 4

(*Through him*)

We keep a close watch on him, but unfortunately, he was able to escape from his nursery.

KRETON

(*Gleefully*)

And you'll never discover how I did *that!*

DELTON 4

(*Unperturbed*)

Knowing his destructive potential, we have been combing the last few hundred years, looking for him. I had only just arrived at the Battle of Waterloo, when I got your message.

ELLEN

I'm very glad you did!

KRETON

Really, Ellen, you sound quite hard. After all, I've done some very nice things while I was here. Ask Mr. Spelding . . . ask the cat. They both liked me a great deal.

ELLEN

And so did I, till you let your hobby get out of hand.

KRETON

It's possible that I *was* overeager, but then that's my nature: work, work, work, morning, noon and night.

DELTON 4

(*To* ELLEN)

Fortunately, it is all over now. And we must go. When we do, time will bend back to the instant before Kreton arrived. It will be as if he'd never come. You will all forget these last few hours.

KRETON

I worked so terribly hard! And now: pouf!

DELTON 4

Let us go, Kreton.

KRETON

(*Scrutinizes* DELTON 4*'s costume*)

And what, may I ask, are you dressed up as?

DELTON 4

I am in the costume of the period. Which is more than I can say for you.

KRETON

Hideously overdressed! And just a bit vulgar . . . like a floor-walker! And as for that ghastly bowler . . .

(DELTON 4 *turns and crosses to the porch door*)

CONRAD

(*To* KRETON)

I hope you aren't going to be in any trouble . . . up there.

KRETON

(*Rising*)

Oh, no. Just a wigging.

DELTON 4

I shall be waiting in the saucer.

(*Goes*)

KRETON

(*Wearily*)

Well, back to the continuum, back to an eternity of ennui. Oh, how I envy you!

CONRAD

For what?

KRETON

For being so violent . . . so loving . . . so beautifully imperfect. And so much happier than you know. Dear girl, think kindly of me . . . until you forget. It's been such fun. For me.

ELLEN

(*Touched*)

Good-by. And I did like you.

DELTON 4

(*Off stage*)

Come, Kreton!

KRETON

(*Conspiratorially*)

But don't worry, I'll be back one bright day. One bright day in 1861. The Battle of Bull Run . . .

DELTON 4

(*Off stage*)

Kreton!

KRETON

(*Gleefully; to* ELLEN)

Only next time I think it'll be more fun if the South wins!

(*With a significant wink, he crosses to the door, waves and exits gaily. As he disappears into the flood of light from the spaceship,* CONRAD *and* ELLEN *go out on the porch and together watch as the spaceships depart in a blaze of light and sound)*

ELLEN

I must say I'm sorry to see him go . . . in a way. (CONRAD *holds her. She sighs happily* ) But now everything's going to be just like it was and . . . (*Sudden horror*) Oh, no!

CONRAD

What's wrong?

ELLEN

Well, when time turns back, we . . . we won't be married. And we won't remember anything.

CONRAD

So we start all over again. Don't worry, honey. I'll see you marry me, somehow.

ELLEN

Oh, darling, I hope so. But you'll have to be firm. I was awfully immature yesterday before I . . . (*With delight*) I saved the world!

(*Time has begun to turn back. Night becomes day.* CONRAD *takes* ELLEN *in his arms. They go off stage.* POWERS *and* ROGER *enter and take up positions exactly as they did in the first scene*)

POWERS

(*Bitterly*)

And it's mine. All of it. The whole insane mess. Of course, when it first broke, it was strictly Strat. Air's baby. Nobody could get near it. Cover them with glory, they thought. Well, I warned them. I said to the Chief of Staff — right in front of Claypoole — I said, "General, mobile laundry units are the coming things . . ."

**CURTAIN**